A-Z *of* Silk Ribbon Flowers

Dedication

For Christian, Alexandria, Rebecca
and Victoria, our very special
grandchildren.

A-Z of Silk Ribbon Flowers

ANN COX

First published in Great Britain 2009

Search Press Limited
Wellwood, North Farm Road,
Tunbridge Wells, Kent TN2 3DR

Text copyright © Ann Cox 2009

Photographs by Debbie Patterson, Search Press Studios; and
Roddy Paine Photographic Studios.
Photographs and design copyright © Search Press Ltd. 2009

The Publishers and author can accept no responsibility for any
consequences arising from the information, advice or instructions
given in this publication.

ISBN: 978-1-84448-199-6

Suppliers
If you have difficulty in obtaining any of the materials and equipment
mentioned in this book, then please visit the Search Press website for
details of suppliers: www.searchpress.com

Alternatively, the author provides her own mail-order service via her
website: www.anncoxsilkribbons.co.uk.

Publishers' note

All the step-by-step photographs in this book feature the author,
Ann Cox, demonstrating how to make silk ribbon flowers. No
models have been used.

Printed in Malaysia.

Acknowledgements

Another big thank you to Roz Dace, who had
faith in my ideas, for commissioning this,
my fourth book. A very special thank you
to Katie Sparkes my editor, not just for her
enthusiasm as new ideas and techniques
developed, but for her endless patience and
humour throughout. She is second to none.
To Juan and Marrianne who made this a
beautiful book and last but certainly not least
– everyone at Search Press, a super team
who support us all.

Contents

The flowers 42

Introduction

As with my previous books, this has been a wonderful adventure. Like an exciting journey, I have planned the route, places to visit and things to do, and then tried to fit everything into a suitcase – or in this case a book. This time, however, I was going to be working on my favourite flowers, life size, but what I did not realise was just how many favourites I had! My aim therefore became to produce a collection of flowers using techniques that would allow other embroiderers not only to reproduce them, but also to use the ideas and techniques to create their own favourite flowers.

This book is for anyone who feels a thrill, a moment of magic, on glimpsing the curve of a petal or the shape of a leaf; who spots a single flower or even a whole bowlful, and wishes they could capture it in stitch. Well now you can, and you do not necessarily have to be an experienced embroiderer – in many cases a single petal or leaf consists of only one stitch when worked in ribbon, and I have graded each flower design according to degree of difficulty, one coloured flower ✿ ✿ ✿ being the easiest and three ✿ ✿ ✿ the most difficult. All I ask is that you follow the step-by-step instructions and have just a little patience when shaping and placing each stitch. This is not as difficult as you might think – the three-dimensional nature of this type of embroidery gives form to the flowers, and is easily controlled by the tension of the stitch. Silk ribbon is available in a variety of widths and a kaleidoscope of colours, and is a very friendly and forgiving medium to work with.

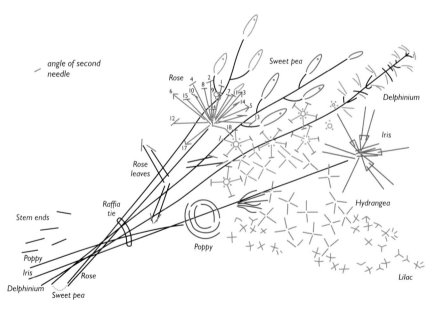

The template for the bouquet shown opposite, reproduced at 40 per cent of its actual size. To enlarge, photocopy at 250 per cent. For instructions on how to transfer the design to your background fabric, see page 20.

A bunch of pink, purple and blue flowers picked from my garden. All of these flowers can be recreated using the designs in this book.

For those of you that are purists, this is not a new method of embroidery, but it is different. Traditional methods of embroidery use threads of every thickness and texture, but what they have in common is that they are all basically round. Ribbon is flat, like a fabric, and this gives the embroiderer the opportunity to create a totally unique, three-dimensional effect. It is only pure silk ribbon that can be threaded into a needle and stitched using traditional embroidery stitches to create the flowers in this book. There are a few basic rules and techniques you will need to learn that are specific to silk ribbon embroidery, particularly if you are new to it or to my methods of working. So please spend a little time to read through the techniques on pages 10–41 before you start. It is essential that the correct size of chenille needle, with its large eye and sharp point, be used with the right width of ribbon, and to know how, where and why to secure the ends of the ribbon, so that it becomes a habit. It should not dampen your enthusiasm, but will increase your understanding of how the ribbon behaves and make the creation of the flower embroideries easier and more fulfilling.

One thing I have learnt over the years is that many embroiderers find the thought of painting the background fabric and the ribbons formidable. Applying paint to a flat surface and making it look life-like is usually the domain of the artist, but I truly urge you to 'have a go'. I promise that, once you have started, you will never look back. Silk ribbon embroiderers have a great advantage over the painter in that they have actually created a three-dimensional version of the flower, making it so much easier to know where to apply the paint.

Pure silk has a unique lustre. It creates its own light and shade, is very easy to paint and can be coloured either before or after it has been worked. Just a touch of paint on the edge of a petal or a vein on a leaf will bring your embroidery to life. Painting the background fabric, with either a light wash or a suggestion of leaves for example, will add depth to the finished embroidery. Keep the colours very pale – more colour can always be added, but it is very difficult to take away. Again, there are a few basic rules to follow, which are fully explained in this book. The correct type of silk or fabric paint must be used and 'fixed' with a medium hot iron. Do not be frightened to mix paint types; I have done so numerous times, but the most important thing is to test the colours on a spare piece of ribbon or fabric before applying them to your work.

All of the flowers in this book are reproduced life size, however those of you that have used my previous books and are familiar with my methods of working will be well aware that each flower can be made smaller by simply working with a narrower ribbon. This will immediately reduce the size of a flower, but a little thought will be needed to scale down the whole composition and I suggest that you work a test flower on a scrap piece of fabric first.

Whatever type or size of flower you choose to embroider, the same principles apply. As all my students will testify, the secret is to observe the real flower in nature and pay attention to detail. For example, make the side stems thinner than the main stem, and for the tiny stems that join the leaves or buds to the side stems, make them thinner still. Look at the shape and form of the stamens in the centre of the flower, or the way the colour of the petals gradually changes towards the centre. These seemingly

Silk ribbon embroidery allows you to create three-dimensional flowers. Needles are used to both stitch and shape the petals and leaves to mimic the actual form of the flower.

Silk ribbon can be painted either before (upper) or after (lower picture) it has been worked.

insignificant details are what defines a really good embroidery, and the added joy is that absolutely no two pieces can ever be exactly the same.

Whatever it was that caught your eye and made you purchase this book, or why it was chosen for you as a gift, my sincerest wish is that it is not left sitting on a shelf collecting dust. I hope that something within these pages will inspire you to gather together some silk ribbons, needles and threads and start to embroider a flower. As you progress, you will be able to develop your own favourite flowers, or perhaps adapt the designs to give them, for example, a Victorian or a contemporary feel. Perhaps you could even invent flowers of your own for a more abstract effect.

Each project has step-by-step instructions that guide you carefully through every stage, together with a template (shown at half of its actual size) and the ribbons, fabrics, threads and paints required. Details of the other materials and equipment you need are given on pages 10–13.

I hope you enjoy this book, and that it will be as much of an adventure for you as it was for me. Like all good adventures, there is no real limit to how far you can go. Never be afraid to experiment, adapt ideas and above all, have fun. Happy sewing!

Instructions for the Aquilegia are provided on pages 44–45. This beautiful flower was created using yellow and green silk ribbon, which was painted before it was worked into straight stitch and ribbon stitch petals and twisted straight stitch spurs. The tips of the stamens were painted orange and the centres of the yellow petals were coloured using a soft orange before the stems and leaves were added to complete the embroidery.

Materials

All you will need are silk ribbons, some fabric and the correct size of chenille needle (depending on the width of ribbon being stitched) in order to start silk ribbon embroidery. You will not need all the items shown over the next few pages, but they all have different uses and you can add to your collection as you progress. You may already have much of what you require, and everything is readily available at most good needlecraft suppliers and by mail order via the internet. Collect threads, interesting pieces of fabric and pictures from magazines or cards as a useful source of inspiration.

Ribbons

Pure silk ribbon is made in a variety of widths: 2, 4, 7 and 13mm are the most frequently used. I also use 32mm wide ribbon occasionally, for example for the Zantedeschia on page 124. There is a vast range of colours to choose from, though not all colours are available in every width. Each colour has a number, and it is a good idea to keep a small sample of each piece of ribbon with the shade number written alongside for reference, though remember that dye lots may vary slightly. Your supplier will probably be only too happy to match a colour if possible, and look out for toned packs and offcuts to increase the range of colours you have to work with. Silk ribbon is washable at low temperatures by hand or on a delicate machine wash.

2mm

4mm

7mm

13mm

2mm

4mm

7mm

13mm

Each of the lilies above has been worked in exactly the same way, but with a different width of ribbon. They are reproduced actual size.

Keep your ribbons in a box to prevent snagging. Make a habit of keeping all your offcuts, anything from 2.5cm (1in), in another box and use these first before cutting a new length. Always use small, sharp scissors and cut the ribbon at an angle. This will prevent the ribbon from fraying and make threading a needle easier.

Fabrics

Like an artist choosing to work on a particular type of paper, I have used a medium-weight linen/cotton fabric, for consistency, throughout this book. Silk ribbon can be embroidered on to any fabric, including silk, cotton, linen, calico, wool, machine-knitted or even card, provided that the fabric supports the type and weight of the embroidery, and the correct size needle for the width of ribbon used can pass through the fabric freely (although occasionally it may be necessary to make a hole first with a pointed tool such as an awl). For instance, working 13mm wide ribbon with a large size 13 needle on a fine silk habitai would need great care, if for no other reason than concealing the anchoring stitches behind the embroidery. I would suggest that you always work on a fabric whose quality warrants the time and expertise required to create the embroidery.

I have used a medium-weight linen/cotton background fabric for all the embroideries in this book.

Tip

When working out the amount of fabric you need, allow a reasonable amount of space around the embroidery and, if you intend to mount and frame your work, add an additional 5cm (2in) to each side. The fabric quantities given for each design in the book allow for mounting and framing, and can be adjusted if necessary.

Threads

You will need a selection of stranded embroidery threads for attaching the ribbon to the background fabric, gathering the ribbon and forming stems and flower centres. As a general rule, a single strand of fabric-coloured thread is used to secure the ribbon to the fabric, and for gathering the ribbon I use a single strand that is the same colour as the ribbon. Other types of thread in a variety of thicknesses and textures are also used for stems and flower centres, such as cotton perle, coton à broder, string, pieces of wool and strips of leather.

Just some of the colours of stranded embroidery thread available.

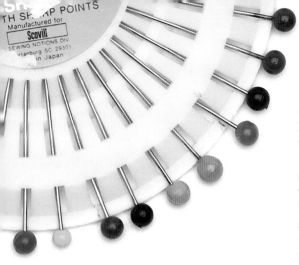

Needles and pins

Chenille needles are the only needles used to embroider with silk ribbon. They have a large eye to accommodate the width of the ribbon and a sharp point, which is essential, and it is important to always use the correct size needle for the width of ribbon being used. The needle must perforate the ribbon easily, and create a hole in the fabric large enough for the ribbon to pass through without being damaged but small enough to hold the ribbon securely so that it can be controlled. I only ever use three sizes of chenille needle: the smallest size 24 for 2mm wide ribbon, the medium size 18 for 4mm and 7mm wide ribbons, and the very large size 13 for 13mm and 32mm widths. A size 8 crewel needle is used for anchoring and gathering threads. I always keep my ribbon embroidery needles separate from the rest of my sewing needles; it is so much easier than searching through each time, and only too easy to accidentally pick up, say, a tapestry needle, which could damage the ribbon if used to stitch through it.

You will also need some pins for supporting the ribbon, once worked, during painting, though avoid passing pins through the ribbon itself. Glass-headed pins are ideal.

2 x No. 13 chenille (for 13 and 32mm ribbon)

2 x No. 18 chenille (for 4 and 7mm ribbon)

2 x No. 24 chenille (for 2mm ribbon)

2 x No. 8 crewel (for embroidery threads)

Tip

When choosing a suitable frame for your embroidery, first cut the required amount of fabric (see page 11) and make sure the frame is large enough for it to fit comfortably inside with at least 2.5cm (1in) around the design. If the embroidery is to be worked on a small but special piece of fabric that is not large enough to put into a frame, extra fabric can be stitched around the outside.

Hoops and frames

Ribbon embroidery, like most other forms of embroidery, is worked in a frame to keep the fabric taut as it is being stitched. Stitching with ribbon is different from thread embroidery in that as the ribbon is pulled through the fabric, the fabric tends to loosen. The type of frame you use is governed by the size of the embroidery and in some cases the type of background fabric used. For smaller projects, I have found the round, plastic flexi frames invaluable as it is so easy to pull the fabric taut, but it is important to remove the frame when not working the embroidery to prevent the fabric from stretching. For larger embroideries, it is more convenient to keep the fabric secured in the frame until the embroidery is complete. For this purpose, adjustable wooden frames (square or rectangular) on which the fabric is secured with silk pins are ideal. It is advisable to tack a piece of waste fabric just outside the picture area to prevent the edge of the fabric becoming soiled as it is worked.

When working on woollen fabrics, care must be taken to prevent it from stretching. Use a wooden frame, either a round or adjustable rectangular type, and bind it with strips of fabric to pad it. Secure the padding, then place the fabric over and secure it evenly but without stretching. Always remove the fabric from the frame when not working the embroidery to prevent stretching.

Painting equipment

There are two basic types of paint used for silk ribbon embroidery, silk paint and fabric paint. Both can be fixed with a medium-hot iron so that the item you have painted is then washable. Silk paint is thin, like water. It spreads easily and rapidly on silk fabric and is perfect for shading petals and leaves. I also use it to shade other fabric backgrounds, provided they are made from a natural fibre, though fabric paint is usually used for this purpose. It is thicker than silk paint and retains the shape of the brushstroke. It is unlikely to run unless it is highly diluted with water.

You only need a few base colours to start with; most other colours can be mixed from these. Invest in some silk paint for shading the ribbon: navy blue, cardinal red and magenta to make beautiful purple tones, and ideally two yellows – primary yellow for a bright green and buttercup yellow for more mossy tones. I also occasionally use raspberry. The fabric paints I use are cardinal red, primary and buttercup yellow, red and cobalt blue.

I often mix fabric and silk paint to obtain the right colour, for example navy blue silk paint mixed with a yellow fabric paint results in a gorgeous green, and I have learnt that it is the thickness of the paint that determines how and if it spreads on the fabric. Fabric paint is ideal for adding fine vein lines and tiny spots of colour to petals and leaves, but always test it on a spare piece of silk ribbon first. Gutta acts as a barrier to stop paint from spreading, but its texture makes it difficult to use for painting very fine lines.

You will also need a smooth, white ceramic tile or a white plate or saucer to mix the paint on; paintbrushes, including a small and a medium coarse, straight-edged brush, and a fine and a medium pointed, round brush. Using a hairdryer will speed up drying time, and is useful for preventing paint from spreading on either the ribbon or the fabric. Small pieces of natural sponge are ideal for lightly painting background foliage, though a small roll of kitchen string is also effective (see Ursinnia, page 112). Experiment, you have nothing to lose, but always test colours first and apply the paint lightly to start with; more colour can always be added.

Other materials and equipment

You will also need a small, sharp pair of scissors, fabric scissors, paper scissors, a fine sharp pencil, a ruler or tape measure, an iron, a hairdryer, tacking cotton and a piece of beeswax or dry soap for waxing threads before stitching stems or stamens. A water pot with a lid and smaller pots with lids are useful for storing water and paint mixes. You will also need paper towels, cotton buds, cocktail sticks, a foam pad and a pith board when painting flowers and leaves; various pieces of string and cord for making stems and branches; clear gutta; medium knitting needles (for forming stamens), small pointed pliers, wadding (for supporting raised petals), interfacing, tweezers, covered florist wires and adhesive.

You will need a small, sharp pair of scissors, fabric scissors, paper scissors, a fine sharp pencil, a ruler or tape measure, an iron, a hairdryer, tacking cotton and a piece of beeswax or dry soap for all the projects in this book. All the other items pictured here can be acquired as and when they are needed, and many of them you are likely to own already.

Painting ribbons

Although there is a vast range of colours to choose from, painting silk ribbon enables the embroiderer to shade and highlight petals and leaves, and to add veins and subtle variations in colour and tone, reflecting the amazing diversity of plants found in nature. It also means that every piece of work will always be unique.

Pure silk is a natural fibre and easy to paint. Generally, silk paint is used, but you will see throughout this book that I have also used fabric paint on certain occasions. Ribbons can be painted before they are worked into an embroidery. Once painted, they can be pressed with a medium-hot iron, after which the ribbon is washable. Both fabric and silk paints can also be used to paint the ribbon after it has been embroidered, but then, of course, it cannot be iron fixed. This is where the different qualities of silk and fabric paint can be put to good use – silk paint is highly fluid, like water, and is perfect for shading the ribbon, while fabric paint is thick and ideal for painting on fine lines such as veins or spots of colour at the centre of a flower where it is vital that the colour does not run.

Mixing paints

Very few paints are required to achieve a broad range of colours and tones. I use navy blue silk paint mixed with either primary yellow or buttercup yellow for two types of green, and add a touch of red for a browner green. Red mixed with a yellow will make numerous shades of orange, and magenta mixed with blue results in beautiful lilacs, mauves and purples. I use opaque fabric paints: white, primary and buttercup yellow, cardinal red and cobalt blue. Colours can be diluted with a little water to make them paler; I always mix my colours a little paler than I think I need, as it is easier to add more colour than to take it away. Never be frightened to experiment with mixing colours, but always test a colour first on a spare piece of ribbon that is the same as the one you are using in your embroidery. Make sure the paint is the right consistency – thin enough to spread freely across the ribbon or, if you are adding details, thick enough not to spread at all. Colours are best mixed on a plain white or pale cream kitchen tile. The paint can dry out quickly, so covering it with a lid from a jar will help to prevent this.

> ### Tip
> Care needs to be taken when painting embroidered ribbon to avoid any colour seeping into the background fabric (see pages 16–17). Moisten the ribbon only, avoid making it too wet, and pick up just a little paint at a time on the brush. Stop painting 3–4mm (about ¼in) from where the ribbon passes through the fabric. A hairdryer can be useful to speed up drying time and prevent the paint from spreading.

These daisies illustrate the range of tones that can be achieved by using different coloured ribbon and shades of paint. Daisies 1, 3 and 4 have each been embroidered using 4mm pink ribbon that has been painted with progressively darker shades of pink silk paint. Flower 2 has been worked in unpainted 4mm dark pink ribbon.

Some of the painting effects you can achieve are shown here. Daisy 1 has been embroidered using randomly painted ribbon (see page 15), creating a patchy effect; a fine line of gutta (though white fabric paint would work just as well) has been painted through the centre of flower 2, allowed to dry then the petals painted a deeper pink; on flower 3 the petals have been shaded from the centre only; and on flower 4 the petals have been shaded at the tip, with just a hint of colour round the centre.

Painting ribbons with silk paint before embroidering

Painting before you stitch allows you to colour the ribbon in different ways, as shown below, to achieve a broad range of finishes in the exact shade or range of tones that you want. After painting, dry the ribbon by suspending it from one end and then press it with a medium-hot iron to fix the colour. This allows you to paint and shade the petals and leaves, once embroidered, to an even finer degree.

For the techniques described over the next few pages, you will need: a small, medium and large straight-edged paintbrush, a fine- and medium-pointed brush, a kitchen tile, a jar for water, pieces of natural sponge and, of course, silk paints.

> **Tip**
>
> If you accidentally apply too much colour, lift off the excess paint by running a piece of absorbent kitchen paper along its length. Alternatively, iron the ribbon between two pieces of absorbent paper with a hot iron, or drop the ribbon into clean water.

Applying paint randomly

This is achieved by dabbing paint on to ribbon that has been loosely crumpled into a loose ball and moistened with clean water. For a more pronounced effect, apply the colour to dry ribbon then add a few drips of water if required. By crumpling together two shades of ribbon, a broad range of tones can be achieved; pink and blue ribbon painted together, for example, work well when used to embroider hydrangeas or lavender.

1. To colour a ribbon two shades of purple, put some blue and magenta silk paint on opposite corners of a glazed tile.

2. Using a medium straight-edged paintbrush, transfer one colour to the other to make two different tones of purple. Dilute with a little water to the required tone.

3. Crumple up the length of ribbon into a loose ball and randomly dab on the two shades of purple paint.

4. Clean the brush, and, if required, drop water into the dry patches to blend the colours.

Blending

To obtain a more subtle, blended effect, you need to tension the ribbon, moisten it and then apply the paint. This results in a more even blend of colours and tones. Always mix your colours before moistening the ribbon to avoid the ribbon drying out.

  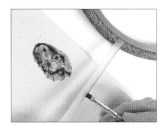

1. Secure the end of the ribbon in a hoop with a weight, such as a book, on top, hold it tautly and moisten it along its length with clean water using a large, flat-ended brush.

2. Use a medium brush to apply the paint. Start at one end, and move towards the other in a single, sweeping movement, lifting the brush off at the end. This creates a subtly blended tone, from dark to light, along the length of the ribbon.

3. To blend the colour from one edge across the width of the ribbon, moisten it across its entire width, and then run paint along the edge using a small, flat-ended brush.

The top ribbon above has been painted so that the colour fades out gradually from left to right (see step 2). The bottom ribbon has had paint applied along the top selvedge and fades out towards the opposite selvedge (see step 3).

Lifting out colour

A less mottled, more shaded effect can also be achieved by painting the ribbon along its length, and then dropping in water to lift out the colour – a clean, dry tissue can also be used.

1. First, moisten the ribbon and apply the paint evenly along its length.

2. While the paint is still wet, drop in spots of clean water. This lifts out the colour, creating a mottled effect.

Using gutta

Gutta acts as a barrier to paint and water. Use it to prevent the paint from spreading, for example to keep the edge of a ribbon its original colour before painting or to create a central, unpainted vein through the centre of a petal or leaf.

1. Apply the gutta straight from the tube along the edge, and allow it to dry thoroughly.

2. Apply paint, taking it up to the edge of the gutta.

Painting veins on leaves

Using fabric paint, which is thicker than silk paint, allows a fine line to be painted on silk with little or no fear of it running, but always test it on a spare piece of silk ribbon first. Use a fine-pointed brush and start at the base of the central vein. Fade out the paint just before the tip, then add the side veins. Veins vary in colour – those of the Fuchsia are red, as in the demonstration below, whereas other flowers, for example Tropaeolum, have paler veins.

1. Mix fabric paint to the required colour and, using a clean, dry, fine-pointed brush, pick up a little paint on the tip. Draw in a fine line from the base of the leaf that fades out just before the tip.

2. Add the side veins, starting at the central vein and fading them out just before the edge of the leaf. Leave to dry.

3. Use the eye-end of a large needle to hold the ribbon up from the fabric, dampen it with clean water and use silk paint to shade it as required. The vein lines will still show clearly.

For pale vein lines, paint on the veins first using white fabric paint and allow to dry, then dampen and use silk paint over the whole leaf with another colour.

16

To obtain a strong, dark central vein along a tall, slender leaf, paint the ribbon before stitching the leaf. Fold the ribbon in half lengthways and iron in the fold before painting.

    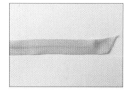

1. Iron a strong central crease along the length of the ribbon.

2. Secure the folded ribbon by pinning it to the edge of a piece of fabric in a hoop, hold it taut and dampen it with a straight-edged brush.

3. Make sure you dampen both sides of the ribbon.

4. Run the colour along the fold using a small, pointed brush and dry it with a hairdryer.

5. Iron the ribbon flat.

Painting flower petals

Petals can be shaded either along the top edge, as shown here, or from the base of the petal towards the edge, depending on the type of flower. In both cases the same principles apply. Use a pointed paintbrush and keep the colour pale, as more colour can always be added. Test it on a spare piece of ribbon first.

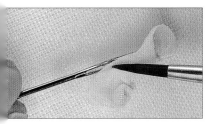  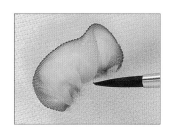

1. Support the petal away from the fabric with the eye-end of a needle and use a fine-pointed brush to moisten the top edge. Avoid making the background fabric wet.

2. Using the same brush, apply a little paint to the moistened edge of the petal. Allow the colour to blend down towards the base of the flower. Repeat if more colour is needed.

3. Apply colour to the base of the petal in the same way.

Tip

To prevent paint spreading into the background fabric:

• if possible, use a hairdryer to dry the paint quickly
• apply a protective layer of gutta to both sides of the fabric, around where the ribbon passes through.

During painting, it is important that the petals or leaves are kept separate to prevent the paint from transferring to another petal or leaf, or to the background fabric. Place a foam pad or sponge, approximately 8–10cm (3–4in) square by 1cm (½in) deep, behind the flower you are painting and use glass-headed pins to keep the petals apart, though avoid passing the pins through the ribbon itself.

1. Place a small foam pad behind the part of the embroidery you are about to paint.

2. Insert glass-headed pins into the foam to hold the petals you are painting away from the rest of the flower and the fabric. Avoid passing the pins through the ribbon.

3. Supporting the petal with the eye-end of a large needle, moisten along the petal edge and allow the moisture to seep downwards.

4. Apply paint along the selvedge of the petal and allow it to spread downwards towards the bottom of the flower. Repeat if more colour is required.

Painting backgrounds

Lightly painting the background fabric before you start to embroider will add another dimension to your work; it will instantly create depth and perspective. I always work with background fabrics made of natural fibres, for example silk, cotton or linen, which can be painted with both silk paint and fabric paint. Silk paint spreads beautifully across the surface of silk, creating gorgeous, subtle tones, whereas it spreads to a much lesser degree on linen and cotton. Fabric paint, which is thicker, retains the shape of the brushstroke and is perfect for background stems and leaves, though it can be diluted to make it spread more readily.

The daisy on the far left has been embroidered on to unpainted fabric; that in the middle has been placed on a subtle background of various shades of green (see below); and that on the right is on a green painted background to which some foliage has been added (see facing page).

Creating a coloured background

To achieve a subtle blend of colours on the fabric, first secure the fabric in an embroidery frame, then mix a range of tones and apply them randomly using a paintbrush, a sponge or even a piece of crumpled, coarse fabric or string. Start by painting the background a little paler than required and build up the colour gradually. When the paint is dry, iron it to fix the colour.

 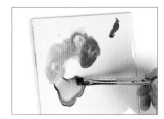 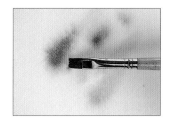 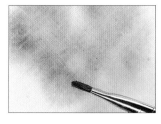

1. Secure the fabric in a hoop, and wet the background using clean water and a large, straight-edged brush.

2. For a green background, mix together blue, yellow and a little red silk paint on a glazed tile to create a range of green tones.

3. Drop the colours at random on to the wet background. Allow them to spread naturally on the fabric.

4. After you have applied the paint, drop in some clean water to diffuse the colour and create a different, more subtle, blended effect.

 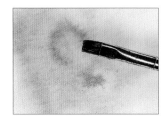 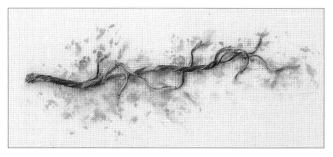

5. To remove paint from areas that are too heavily coloured, blot with a crumpled piece of paper towel.

6. Add another colour at this stage if you wish to, applying it in the same way and dropping in water to diffuse it if necessary.

This mottled background was created by picking up a little fabric paint using a slightly damp, torn section of natural sponge and lightly dabbing different tones of green on to a dry background. Always apply the lighter tones first, and progressively introduce darker ones. This sample is on a linen/cotton fabric, but the same effect can be achieved on silk if the paint is applied very gently.

Leaves, branches and background foliage

Adding painted leaves, branches and foliage to your background can give your finished embroidery depth and perspective. On the left, the string branch was attached first and then a few, pale background leaves were lightly painted in. The foreground flower and foliage were then embroidered, creating the overall illusion of a wide, spreading branch. Contrast this with the branch at the bottom of page 18. The mottled background suggests much denser, more distant foliage, increasing the illusion of depth.

Use fabric paints for background leaves as they will not run, though I often mix navy blue silk and yellow fabric paint for particularly pleasing greens. Keep the mix thick and test it on a piece of spare fabric first to make sure it does not run. Always work on a dry background, use the minimum of paint on your brush and apply the brushstrokes lightly; more colour can always be added but it cannot be removed.

Leaves

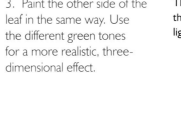

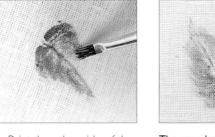

1. Mix navy blue silk paint with yellow and a touch of red fabric paint to make two or three greens, and paint in a central vein that fades towards the tip with a single sweep of a small, straight-edged brush.

2. Lightly paint one side of the leaf using small brushstrokes that curve outwards and upwards from the centre vein, all in the same direction, suggesting the shape of the leaf.

3. Paint the other side of the leaf in the same way. Use the different green tones for a more realistic, three-dimensional effect.

The completed leaves. See how the brushstrokes, although very light, suggest a leaf that curves.

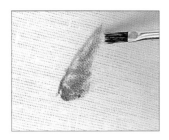

Leaves vary greatly in shape, size and colour. Refer to the actual leaves or a photograph for guidance.

Grass stems

Branches

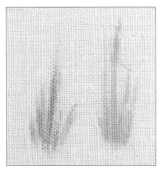

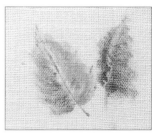

Paint grass stems using single strokes of the brush worked from the base of the stems upwards. Lift the brush gradually as it progresses to the tip to create a tapered leaf.

Completed grass stems. Vary the tone and the widths of the leaves for a more interesting and realistic effect.

Using a fine brush draw in a fine, slightly ragged line for the top and bottom edges of the main branch and add the side branches and twigs. Apply paint randomly using different shades of green and brown to colour the branch.

Transferring the design

Before transferring the design to the fabric, cut the fabric to the appropriate size (see page 11) and secure in an embroidery frame or hoop (see page 12). If you are using a square embroidery frame, check that the grain of the fabric is straight then secure it with silk pins to prevent the fabric from becoming damaged. Note that if the background is to be painted, do this before transferring the design.

1. Place the frame centrally under the fabric, tension it across the shortest width in the centre and secure with silk pins. Tension across the centre of the longest width and secure as before.

2. Check that the grain of the fabric is straight then continue pinning along opposite sides of the fabric, working outwards from the central pins at approximately 4cm (1½in) intervals.

The completed frame.

The templates

The structure of the flowers embroidered in this book varies greatly; some, like the Ursinnia below (see page 112), have petals consisting of simple straight stitches, whereas others, such as the Chrysanthemum (page 50) are more complex. For this reason, I have included a template with each design that will enable you to transfer accurately most if not all of the various elements on to the fabric. The templates show the start, finish and direction of the main stitches, including petals, leaves, buds and stems, as well as the position and angle of a second needle that is used to control the ribbon as the stitch is formed. Although colour has been used to distinguish the different elements, only a black and white photocopy is required for the purposes of transferring the design (see page 21).

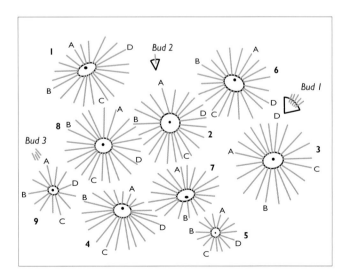

20

Begin by photocopying the template, enlarged to twice its size, then draw a rectangular border around the outside and cut it out on the line. Place the template in the centre of the fabric, making sure that it is placed on the straight of the grain, and secure with a pin on each side. As your embroidery is being worked, the edges of the fabric can become soiled. Always wash your hands first, of course, but it advisable to also protect the fabric using a frame of thin cotton fabric. When the embroidery is complete, the protective frame can be kept for future use.

1. Cut out a frame for your embroidery from a piece of scrap fabric. The centre should be slightly bigger than the template, and the border not less than 5cm (2in) wide.

2. Pin the template in the centre of the fabric and tack closely around the edge of (though not through) the template using a light-coloured thread.

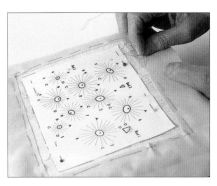

3. Pin the fabric frame over the top and tack it in position. You are now ready to transfer the design.

4. Following the instructions provided with the template, transfer flowers 2 to 5 by making a hole through the template and the fabric at each end of each petal using a size 18 needle.

5. Using a propelling pencil (or a sharp, fine pencil), go through each hole in the template to make a dot on the fabric underneath.

Tip

At times you may need to lift up the template to check or transfer part of the design. To replace it accurately within its tacked boundary, put pins through the holes in the template and the corresponding marks in the fabric, and secure with two pins while you check or add to the design.

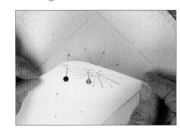

6. Unpin the lower edge and the sides of the template, roll it back and secure it with a pin. Be careful not to move the template as you will need to replace it in exactly the same position to transfer the rest of the design.

7. Very lightly draw in the flower centres and the lines connecting the two ends of the petals marked A to D.

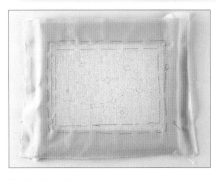

8. Replace the template and transfer the rest of the design in the same way. Remove the template.

Basic ribbon techniques

The secret of successful silk ribbon embroidery is to master a few basic techniques, which are explained below, and make maximum use of the width and lustre of the ribbon for every stitch worked. As a fibre, silk is extremely strong, however when woven into ribbon and stitched, it deteriorates slightly each time it passes through the fabric. For this reason you should always work with a short length of ribbon and use the correct size of chenille needle for the width of ribbon being used (see page 12). Typically, I would recommend using 33cm (13in) or less, but there are projects in this book where I suggest a different length to prevent wastage.

Cutting and threading the ribbon

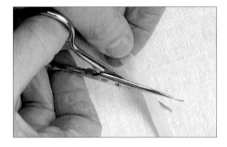

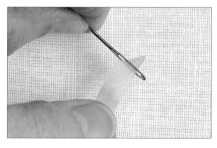

1. Cut the ribbon using a small pair of sharp scissors. Always cut at an angle, as this will prevent fraying and makes it easier to thread the needle. The angled cut end of the ribbon is referred to as the tag end.

2. Smooth the ribbon by pulling it under a medium-hot iron. Though not always essential, this is well worth doing and will restore the original lustre of the silk.

3. Thread the ribbon, pointed end first, through the eye of the needle.

Folding ribbon to shape a petal or leaf

Some stitches require you to fold the ribbon lengthways before threading it through the needle. This is used for flowers whose petals have an elongated throat, for example nasturtiums.

1. Fold the ribbon in half lengthways and pass it through the eye of the needle, with the fold at the bottom.

2. Take it through to the back of the fabric, retaining the fold, and anchor it in position (see page 23 opposite).

The Tropaeolum flowers on page 108 were worked in straight stitch (see page 26), starting with a folded ribbon, as shown on the left.

Anchoring the ribbon

The technique for anchoring wide ribbon (7, 13 and 32mm) to the fabric is different from that for narrow ribbon (2 and 4mm). For all widths of ribbon, start by anchoring the ribbon behind where the first stitch is to be worked using a fabric-coloured thread. Always avoid embroidering through any ribbon on the wrong side – as the ribbon is pulled through, the stitches on the right side will be destroyed. If necessary, use the needle to make a hole right through the fabric from the back first to find the best route through.

Anchoring 2mm and 4mm ribbon

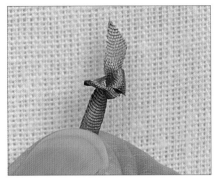

1. Tie a single loose knot in the end of the ribbon.

2. Tighten the knot by sliding the ribbon between your forefinger and thumb to push the knot to the end.

3. Thread the ribbon into a needle and bring it up through to the front of the fabric so that the knot is at the back. Trim off any excess ribbon.

Anchoring 7mm and 13mm ribbon

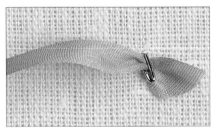

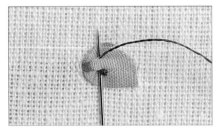

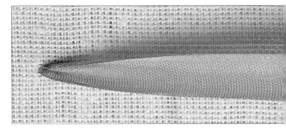

1. Thread the short side of the ribbon tag end into a needle and take the needle through to the back of the fabric.

2. Anchor the tag end left at the back of the fabric with two or three small stitches, depending on the width of the ribbon. (32mm ribbon will require two or more stitches worked across the width of the ribbon to retain the shape of the ribbon on the right side.) Use a single strand of fabric-coloured thread (I have used a coloured thread here for clarity).

3. Turn the fabric over to the right side and look at the shape of the ribbon where it comes through the needle hole in the fabric. Here, both edges are curling upwards to form a trough and there is a small fold along the top edge. This will need to be turned.

> *Tip*
>
> When working with a large (size 13) needle, always try to pass the needle between the fabric threads rather than through them to avoid damaging the fabric.

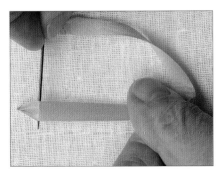

4. First turn the ribbon over to unwind it so that the edges of the ribbon curl down to the fabric.

5. Hold the ribbon taut and slide the eye-end of a needle firmly along the underside of the ribbon, to the point where it comes up through the fabric, to 'iron' it. While the ribbon is flat across its width, work the first stitch, shaping and stitching as required.

Controlling the ribbon

Ribbon can become twisted as you work, in which case you will need to untwist and iron it (see page 23). There may be times, however, when you require a twisted ribbon, for example when stitching Monarda petals (see page 28).

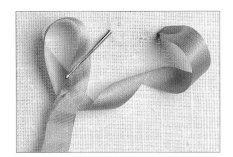

A twisted ribbon, with the needle in the fabric ready to work a straight stitch.

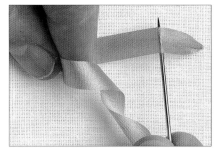

1. Untwist the ribbon where it comes up through the fabric and iron it (see page 23, steps 3–5) (this is the area that will form the stitch, up to where it is being held by the needle).

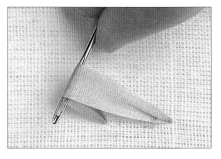

2. Replace the sewing needle with the eye-end of a second needle to pull the ribbon over as you form the stitch, maintaining the tension as you do so.

Fastening off a stitch

It is important to fasten the ribbon off frequently to avoid taking the needle through any ribbon at the back of the embroidery. The needle will pass through the ribbon easily, but as it is pulled through it will destroy the stitches worked on the front of the fabric. Always use a single strand of fabric-coloured thread and secure the end of the ribbon with a few small stitches. Position these behind and within the boundary of the last stitch or stitches worked, as all untidy ends will show through at the front of the embroidery.

The two widest ribbons (13 and 32mm) must in most cases be fastened off after each stitch is worked. This ensures that each stitch is positioned accurately, prevents too much bulk at the back of the fabric, and avoids accidentally stitching through the ribbon. It is also a far speedier method of working and is a more efficient use of ribbon.

Work two or three small stitches across the width of the ribbon, taking care not to pass the thread through the ribbons on the front of the embroidery. Use a single strand of fabric-coloured thread (a contrasting thread is used here for clarity).

Working with 13mm and 32mm ribbon

When working with a large size 13 chenille needle, try to pass the point of the needle between the threads of the fabric and move the needle around in the fabric to make a slightly larger hole. If using a very fine fabric, I suggest that you work a stitch or two on a small piece of spare fabric to test if it is suitable for use with such a large needle and wide ribbon. Fold the ribbon to thread it into a needle and secure the end, then use a cotton bud to shape the petal, as shown below.

1. To pass the ribbon through the fabric, fold it lengthways without creasing and pass it through the eye of a size 13 needle.

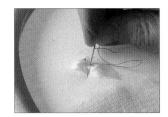

2. On the back of the fabric, open the ribbon out and work a few small stitches across the width of the ribbon using a fabric-coloured thread and secure it directly behind the stitch about to be worked. A contrasting thread is used here for clarity.

3. To accentuate the hollow at the base of a petal, tension the ribbon and shape it with a cotton bud. (Moistening the ribbon first may make this easier.) To form a different type of petal, use the cotton bud to shape it on the underside.

4. Shape the tip of the petal over a cotton bud as you gently pull the ribbon through the fabric to the back.

Rectifying mistakes

The secret of silk ribbon embroidery is to make full use of the width of the ribbon, to retain the lustre of the ribbon and to keep stitches crease free. If you use the correct size needle (see page 12) and follow the instructions on pages 22–25, there is no reason why you should not be able to produce successful embroideries. However, mistakes do happen, and on this page I will explain how the more common ones can be rectified. Most problems occur while tensioning the ribbon to create a petal or leaf; the feel of the ribbon as it is pulled through the fabric is different from that of pulling through a thread, so watch the back of the fabric to prevent the ribbon from being pulled through too far and over-tightening the stitch at the front. If a stitch needs to be unpicked, place the point of a needle in the ribbon where it last went down through the fabric and lift it back up. Never place the eye of a needle in the loop of the stitch to lift it as it will pull the stitches just worked tight and 'iron in' creases.

Ribbon twisting on back of work

Ribbon that has become twisted at the back of the fabric will result in the ribbon being rolled where it comes through at the front of the fabric. (See also 'Controlling the ribbon', page 24.)

Ribbon twisted at the back of the fabric.

Rolled ribbon where it comes up through the front of the fabric.

1. Use the point of a needle to pull the ribbon through to the back of the fabric a little way.

2. Flatten the part of the ribbon that will remain on the back by tensioning it over the eye-end of a needle, then pull the twisted section back through to the front.

Ribbon pulled through too tightly

Ribbon that is pulled through to the back of the fabric too tightly will roll up, become creased and lie flat against the fabric. Never place the eye-end of a needle under the stitch to lift it back as this will immediately tighten the stitches just worked and 'iron' in creases.

 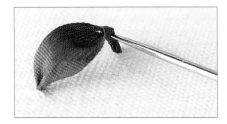 

Ribbon that has been pulled through the fabric too tightly.

1. Put the point of a needle into the ribbon where it goes down through the fabric and lift it back up a short way.

2. Open out the stitch and gently pull the ribbon through to the back over the eye-end of a second needle to re-form the stitch.

Ribbon worked using running stitch

Ribbon should always be worked using a stab stitch technique, never running stitch, to prevent the ribbon from becoming twisted. Each stitch is, in fact, a straight stitch.

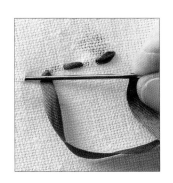 

Ribbon worked as a running stitch will twist and compress (right). Always use a stab stitch technique – take the ribbon through the fabric once only and tension each stitch over the eye-end of a needle before moving on to the next (far right).

Straight stitch

This is a very simple stitch that can be used in a great many different ways. As with all silk ribbon embroidery, the effect created is governed by the width of the ribbon being used, the length of the stitch and the tension of the ribbon as the shape of the stitch is formed over the eye-end of a second needle. A stitch can start from either the base or the tip of a petal or leaf. It can be a loop, as used for the Delphinium (see page 56) or twisted several times to curl the petal, as for the monarda (see page 82). An important point to remember is that the behaviour of the ribbon at the point where it comes up through the fabric is different from that where it goes back down.

Rounded petals and leaves

To begin, anchor the ribbon at the base of the stitch, re-thread it into a needle and take the needle back down through the fabric at the tip of the petal or leaf. (See also looped ribbon stitch, page 31.)

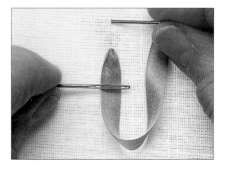

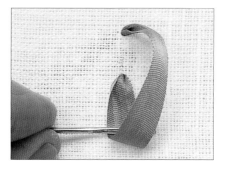

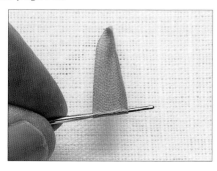

1. Use a second needle to 'iron' the ribbon first (see page 23 steps 4 and 5). Hold the ribbon flat on the fabric under the eye-end of the second needle, then take the needle and ribbon back down through the fabric.

2. Pull the ribbon through, guiding it over the second needle. This helps shape the stitch and keeps the ribbon flat.

3. As the loop tightens around the needle, lift the needle off the surface of the fabric. Keep the ribbon tight over the needle as it is pulled through to the back.

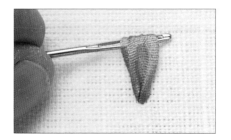

4. Gradually take the second needle up towards the top of the stitch and, keeping the tension of the ribbon over the needle, pull the ribbon at the back towards the base of the stitch. Stop pulling immediately the stitch is formed and remove the needle to create a rounded edge at the top.

The finished stitch.

Pointed petals and leaves

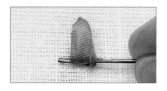

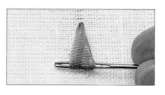

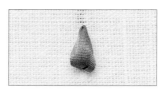

1. To create a pointed petal or leaf, tighten the ribbon as before, but this time with the second needle positioned at the top of the petal.

2. Gradually pull the needle back towards the base of the stitch as you continue to tighten the ribbon.

3. Pull the ribbon away from the base of the stitch as you pull it through to elongate the stitch and create a point.

The finished stitch.

To curve the tip of a leaf or petal to the right, hold the second needle at a 45° angle to pull the stitch out to the left, and pull the ribbon out towards the right underneath the fabric. To curve the stitch to the left, angle the second needle out to the right and pull the ribbon underneath through to the left.

To curve the tip of a leaf or petal to the right, hold the second needle in the loop at the angle shown above, tensioning the stitch to the left, and pull the ribbon to the right underneath the fabric.

The completed stitch, curved to the right.

To curve a stitch to the left, angle the second needle the opposite way, and pull the ribbon underneath the fabric to the left.

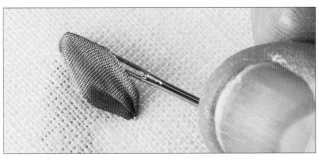

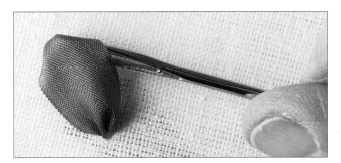

To create an even sharper point, with less fullness at the base of the stitch, tension the tip of the petal over the eye-end of a large needle.

When using wider ribbon (13mm wide and over), use either the end of a large size 13 needle, or a cotton bud to shape the tip of the petal.

Tip

The direction in which you pull the ribbon underneath the fabric while forming a stitch will affect the shape of the finished petal or leaf.

1. While tensioning the stitch by pulling the loop back away from the base of the stitch using the eye-end of a needle, pull the ribbon underneath the fabric away from the stitch.

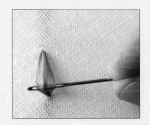

For a more pointed tip, repeat step 2, but this time, just as the stitch is formed, pull the ribbon underneath the fabric back past the bottom of the stitch and move the needle to the base. This shifts the fullness to the base of the petal.

2. Continue to pull the ribbon through, then just as the stitch is formed, stop pulling and remove the needle. This results in the petal having a rounded tip.

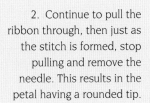

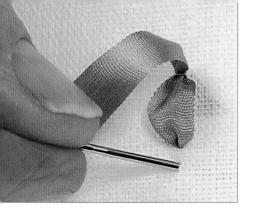

Pad stitch

A pad stitch is simply a straight stitch that is a little shorter than and worked underneath the main stitch. This gives the stitch more bulk and fullness. It is often used for the ovary at the base of a rose, for example.

Forming a stitch over a pad stitch.

Twisted straight stitch

Some flowers have twisted petals, like the Chrysanthemum on page 53 or the Monarda on page 82 (and shown below), that twist and turn in different directions. Most petals of this type are worked with either 2 or 4mm ribbon, but this will depend on the size and variety of flower. The spurs of the Aquilegia on page 44 (and shown at the bottom of the page) are twisted and shaped like a cone, and are worked with 7mm ribbon.

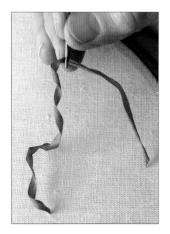

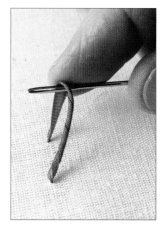

1. Using either 2 or 4mm ribbon, bring it up through to the front of the fabric at the base of the petal and twist it several times.

2. Hold the twists in place over the eye-end of a needle. As you pull it through the fabric, ease the coils towards the start of the stitch and hold them in place.

The completed twisted straight stitch. This can be allowed to bend and curl, depending on the flower being worked.

The Monarda (see page 82). Twisted straight stitch has been used for the pink petals at the top of the flower.

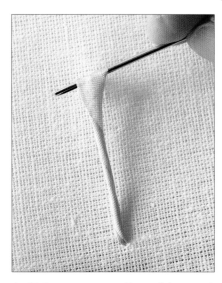

1. To form a spur, use 7mm ribbon, and untwist the top of the stitch to flatten it over the eye-end of a needle so that it is wider at the top than at the bottom.

2. Using a toning thread, put a small stitch at the top of the spur to retain the width and, if necessary, hold it in place.

The Aquilegia. Twisted straight stitch has been used for the spurs at the base of each flower and the main bud.

Ribbon stitch

This is the one stitch that cannot be used in any other form of embroidery. Ribbon has width and is, in effect, a fabric, and when threaded into a needle it can be stitched through itself anywhere across its width. It is ideal for creating flowers and foliage in beautiful, three-dimensional form. The stitch is shaped, then the needle is taken through the ribbon to the back of the fabric. As the ribbon is pulled through it forms a loop at the front, into which a second needle can be placed to pull the ribbon over. As the ribbon is gently pulled through, a roll is created round the needle at the front, forming a perfect edge for petals and leaves. As with all silk ribbon embroidery, tension is critical and will depend on the width of the ribbon being used and the size of the flower worked.

Centre ribbon stitch

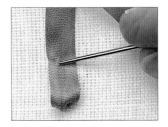   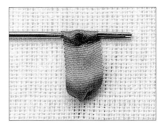

1. Anchor the ribbon and flatten it (see page 23), then give it a slight lift to shape it. Place the point of the needle in the centre of the ribbon at the tip of the stitch, then take the needle through to the back of the work.

2. Carefully pull the ribbon through. If the ribbon starts to twist, straighten it by guiding it over the eye-end of a second needle (see page 25).

3. To make a rounded tip to a leaf or petal, lay the eye-end of a second needle across the ribbon inside the loop, at the point where the ribbon passes through to the back of the fabric.

4. Continue pulling the ribbon round the needle. Keeping this needle in place, either bring the sewing needle up for the next stitch or fasten off behind the stitch. Remove the second needle.

Tip
Unless stated otherwise, the second needle used to shape the petal should be the same size as the one used to stitch the ribbon.

The completed ribbon stitch.

To create a more pointed tip, remove the second needle at step 4, then very gently pull the ribbon through and stop pulling immediately a point is formed.

Reverse centre ribbon stitch

Many petals curve backwards, for example rose petals, and reversing the above method is one way of achieving this.

1. Place the ribbon as in step 1, fold it at an angle and place the point of the needle through it under the centre of the fold. Take it down through the ribbon and fabric to the back, using either the eye-end of a second needle or a cotton bud placed in the point to gently pull the ribbon over.

The completed reverse centre ribbon stitch.

Left and right ribbon stitch

These variations of the basic ribbon stitch are used to create a pointed leaf or petal that curves to either the left or the right.

  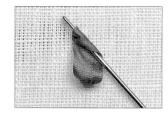 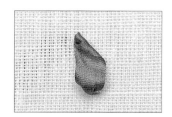

1. To create a stitch with a rolled edge that curves to the left, take the needle through the left edge of the ribbon.

2. Place the eye-end of a second needle at an angle in the loop of the ribbon and start to gently pull the ribbon through.

3. Continue to pull the ribbon to shape it round the eye-end of a second needle, then either leave this needle in place as you start the next stitch or fasten off.

The completed left ribbon stitch.

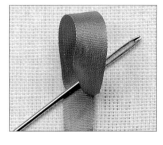 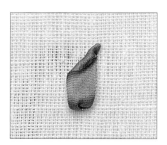

1. To create a rolled stitch that curves to the right, take the needle down through the right edge of the ribbon, and lay the second needle in the opposite direction (shown left). Tighten the ribbon and continue as before.

The completed right ribbon stitch.

Reverse left and right ribbon stitch

This stitch is used for some petals that fold backwards or under, for example the Chrysanthemum (page 50).

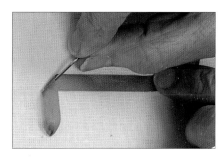 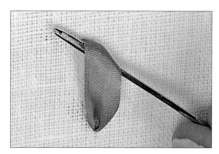 

1. To create a reverse ribbon stitch curved to the left, fold the ribbon over the needle at the top of the stitch so that the ribbon forms a right angle. Keeping the needle in the same position, take it through the ribbon at the lower left edge of the fold.

2. Partly pull the ribbon through, then place the eye-end of a second needle at the angle shown above and continue to gently pull the ribbon to form a backward-facing roll. Stop pulling immediately the stitch is formed.

The completed reverse left ribbon stitch.

  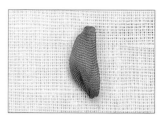

Step 1

Step 2

The completed reverse right ribbon stitch.

A reverse right ribbon stitch is formed in the same way as a reverse left ribbon stitch, but with the ribbon curved in the opposite direction.

Folded ribbon stitch

This stitch gives a folded edge to a petal and is worked mainly in 4 and 7mm ribbon. Either edge can be folded over as far as you wish to either the right or the left. Folded versions of reverse ribbon stitch can also be worked.

Pick the edge of the ribbon up from the underside with the point of the needle, lift and fold the ribbon over, then take the needle back down through the ribbon. Pull the ribbon gently through to complete the stitch.

The completed ribbon stitch, folded to the left.

A completed right folded ribbon stitch.

Looped ribbon stitch

This stitch gives more depth and fullness to a flower, such as a Delphinium (see page 56). The distance between the point at which the ribbon comes up through the fabric and where it goes back down can vary, as can the height of the loop. Also, the needle can go through the ribbon at either the front or the back of the petal. Here, the ribbon stitch is worked at the front to give a narrow throat to the petal.

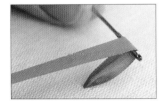

1. Bring the ribbon through to the front of the fabric and form a loop over the eye-end of a second needle.

2. Retain the tension on the loop and take the ribbon back down just below the base of the stitch (but not through the same hole).

3. Pull the ribbon through to form the looped ribbon stitch.

For a flatter loop, take the ribbon back down a little further from the point at which you brought it through to the front.

Double ribbon stitch

This type of stitch is useful for making flower parts that have an elongated, slender tip, such as the calyxes in the rose project on page 102. Here I have used 7mm ribbon.

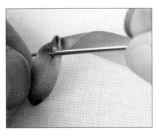

1. Place the ribbon as for a ribbon stitch, but do not take the needle through the ribbon or the fabric.

2. Keep the needle in the same place but lift it out of the fabric and pull it through the ribbon.

3. Still hold the ribbon flat and pull the ribbon tight to form a ribbon stitch.

4. Take the needle through the ribbon again, just below the point at which it went through for the first stitch.

5. Hold the ribbon flat and pull it through to form a double ribbon stitch.

The completed double ribbon stitch (right), and the same stitch made with 4mm ribbon (far right).

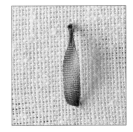

Gathering techniques

The fineness of silk ribbon allows it to be gathered to great effect, allowing you to create a completely different range of flowers. The effect created will depend on the width of the ribbon, the length of the ribbon gathered and the placement of the running stitches. The stitches should be very tiny, 1–2mm (about ¹⁄₁₆in), and worked on the selvedge to create a frill with a smooth flair. Longer stitches create a frill that undulates, making it more difficult to attach to the fabric. The demonstration below is for a small, very simple flower, such as a blossom. There are numerous variations on this basic technique, which will be explained in the individual flower sections.

Always gather the ribbon with a ribbon-coloured thread and secure it to the fabric with a fabric-coloured thread so that each thread can be identified. A contrasting thread has been used in the demonstration below for clarity. If the flower and the fabric are the same colour, gather the ribbon with a very pale, different shade of thread. It is important to cut the ribbon at an angle and to start the stitching 1cm (½in) from the tag end.

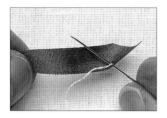

1. Thread a strand of ribbon-coloured thread into a fine needle and knot one end. Bring the needle up through the selvedge, on the long side of the ribbon, 1cm (½in) from the end, then work a second stitch over the edge to secure it.

 Tip

Work tiny stitches. Stitches that are too long will create an undulating frill, like the one shown here, rather than a flared one. This type of frill is also more difficult to attach to the fabric.

2. Work a line of tiny running stitches, about 1mm (¹⁄₁₆in) long, across the ribbon, at the same angle as the tag end (45°).

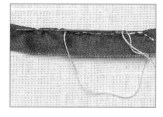

3. Continue to work running stitches along the selvedge for approximately 5cm (2in); the longer the gathered edge, the larger the flower.

4. Now stitch back across the ribbon at a 45° angle to the running stitches as before, unthread the needle but do not cut the thread, then cut the ribbon across at the same angle 1cm (½in) from the stitch line as before.

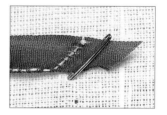

5. To anchor the ribbon, thread the tag end into a needle so that the eye is parallel with the stitching and cut line, as shown above.

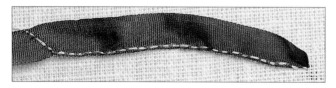

6. Hold the ribbon firmly in place on the fabric then pull the needle and tag end through the fabric so that the diagonal line of stitching lies completely within the line of the fabric, and is not visible on either side. Anchor the ribbon on the back of the fabric using a fabric-coloured thread, underneath where the petal will lie and close to where the ribbon comes through the fabric. Make sure you do not stitch through the gathering thread.

 Tip

When anchoring the ribbon, do not position the needle vertically relative to the diagonal stitching (as shown opposite). If the needle is pulled through with the needle in this position, the diagonal stitching line will sit either side of the fabric and show on the front.

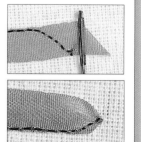

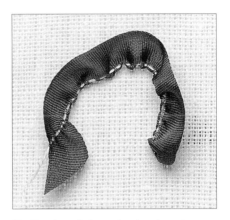

Tip

Be careful not to pass the needle through the tag end of the ribbon already anchored at the back of the fabric.

7. Gently pull the gathering thread to just slightly gather the ribbon, and begin to shape it round.

8. Take the needle part way back down through the fabric, as close as possible to where the ribbon comes up. Thread the loose end of the ribbon into a needle, ensuring the stitching lies parallel to the eye of the needle, as before.

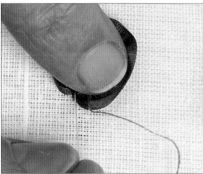

9. Take the ribbon through to the back of the fabric, as before, so that none of the diagonal stitching shows on either side of the fabric. Leave the gathering thread showing at the front of the fabric. Anchor the ribbon as before.

10. Bring the anchoring thread (the blue thread in the picture above) through to the front of the fabric, close to where the ribbon goes through.

11. Lightly place your finger in the centre of the ribbon, and gently pull the gathering thread with your other hand. This helps to gather the ribbon evenly. Check the centre hole and continue gathering until it is the correct size.

12. Using the blue anchoring thread, and without stitching through the gathering stitches, work small stitches over the gathering line around the centre to secure. Fasten off at the back of the fabric.

13. Place your finger over the centre of the flower as before, and gently pull the gathering thread again to seat the gathers. Fasten off the thread at the back of the fabric.

14. Place a French knot in the centre to complete the flower.

Tip

When pulling the tag end of a gathered ribbon through the fabric, place your index finger on the gathered section and hold it firmly in place as you pull the end through the fabric. Generally the stitch line will then sit accurately within the line of the fabric.

French knots

French knots embroidered in ribbon create a totally different effect, adding yet another dimension to silk ribbon embroidered flowers. Again, it is the width of the ribbon, the number of loops worked and, in particular, the tension applied to the knot which determines the effect created, as is shown in the sample below right. French knots are frequently used in conjunction with petalled flowers, for example Buddleia (page 48), to suggest roundness and depth, or a spray of flowers, for example Crambe (page 54). It is also particularly useful for distant flowers, for example a pillar of roses, as part of a background or a small arrangement.

Tip

When making French knots, never wind the ribbon flat around the needle as in the picture below; always put a twist in it, as shown in the demonstration.

Tip

If you are left-handed, hold the needle in your left hand as you would normally, twist the ribbon once anti-clockwise and proceed as in step 2 but from the left.

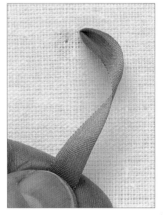

1. Anchor the ribbon, and turn it once, clockwise, to put a twist in it.

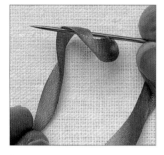

2. Take the ribbon over to the left, and, keeping hold of it, wrap it loosely around the needle once.

3. Wrap it twice more, as shown, or the number of times required to make the size of knot you need.

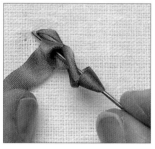

4. Place the needle in the fabric, close to the point where it came up through the fabric.

5. Hold the needle upright and slide the coils of ribbon down towards the fabric. At the same time, gently pull the ribbon through. Tension the ribbon sufficiently to form the size of knot you require.

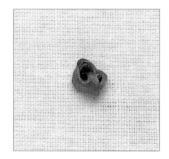

6. Take the needle and ribbon down through the fabric. Stop pulling the ribbon when the knot is the correct size and shape.

This sample illustrates the approximate size of French knot created using different width ribbons and varying the number of loops worked round the needle. From bottom to top, the rows are worked using 2mm, 4mm, 7mm and 13mm ribbon, with the first knot on the left worked with one loop, the centre one with two loops and the one on the right with three loops.

Lazy daisy stitch

Also known as detached chain stitch, lazy daisy stitch is an easy and very useful stitch. It can be used to work smaller, different-sized irises, for example; as part of a flower, as in the Wisteria; or for buds on the side of a stem. It is essential to always work the stitch using the stab stitch technique shown below, otherwise the stitch loses its depth and form. The tension of the loop is governed by the size of the stitch and the width of ribbon.

The top petal of this iris was created using lazy daisy stitch.

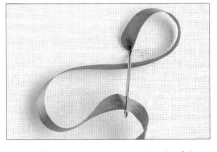

1. Anchor the ribbon at the back of the fabric, and take the needle back down through the fabric as close as possible to where it came up.

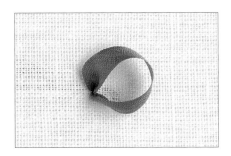

2. Pull the ribbon through and leave a loop. Guide the ribbon over your finger or a needle to keep the ribbon from twisting.

3. Bring the needle back up just inside the top of the loop. Adjust the size of the loop and take it back down on the other side, close to where the ribbon comes up through.

4. Place the eye-end of a second needle in the loop to keep the ribbon flat as it is pulled through.

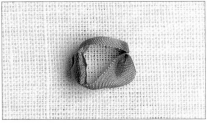

5. Stop pulling the ribbon through when it sits evenly over the loop without flattening it. Remove the second needle to complete the stitch.

Tip

Avoid pulling the second loop, which holds the first loop in place, too tight, as it is the width of this ribbon that keeps the first loop open and shapes the petal. Also, if the second loop is over-tightened it will be more visible.

Open lazy daisy stitch

This can be used in the same context as the lazy daisy stitch above, to suggest a partly open bud or a small iris.

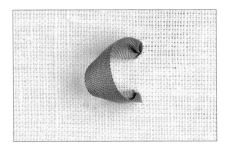

1. Begin the stitch as before, but form a loop by taking the needle back down a little distance away from where it came up through the fabric.

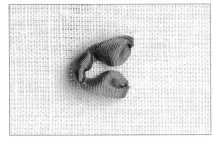

2. Complete the stitch as before.

Using threads

You will need a variety of threads, in different thicknesses and textures, for flower centres, stems, grasses, background leaves, twigs and branches (see page 11). They can be used to great effect using just a few basic stitches, which are described on the following pages. I always pull stranded threads separately for stems, then reassemble them using the number of strands required for the thickness of stem, and using different mixes of colours to produce light and shade.

Fly stitch

This is a useful stitch, often used for the calyx of a small flower, tiny leaves or even conifer. It can also be worked in ribbon to great effect.

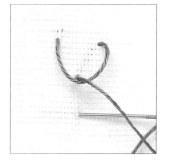

1. Form an open loop, and secure it with a stitch over the loop that extends to form a stem.

2. Tighten the thread to complete the stitch.

To create a leaf, work several fly stitches in a row from the tip downwards, shaping and curving them as you go.

French knots

This stitch, worked using a strand of thread, is useful when a tiny French knot is required (that is, smaller than a French knot worked with 2mm ribbon). It is most often used for stamens and flower centres, and could be used for flowers like the Crambe (page 54) to suggest more distant or smaller flowers.

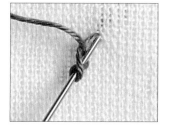

Bring the thread up to the front of the fabric, wrap it around the needle a few times (usually between one and eight times, depending on the size of the knot required) and then take it back down close to where the needle came up through the fabric.

Pistil stitch

A pistil stitch is worked like a French knot, except that the needle is taken down through the fabric a short distance away from the start point to form a stalk. It is often combined with French knots as shown below. It can also be worked in ribbon.

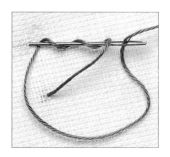

1. Pistil stitches are formed the same as French knots (see above), except that the needle is taken back through the fabric a short distance away from the point where the needle came up.

2. Pull the needle through and tighten the knot to complete the stitch.

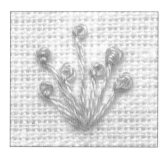

A group of pistil stitches that radiate out from the centre of a flower.

Here, French knots and pistil stitches have been combined to form a flower centre composed of stamens, suggesting that each is on a short stem.

Flower centres

Flower centres vary greatly and it is important to replicate them as accurately as possible in order to create a life-like flower. The centre of a flower is made up of stamens and sometimes a pistil. The densely packed, short stamens found in the centre of a daisy can be re-created using French knots, and different effects can be achieved by varying the size of the French knots and colour of the threads used, as shown below. In this section I demonstrate a number of basic techniques suitable for a wide range of flowers; variations on these are explained in the individual flower sections.

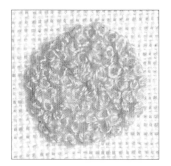 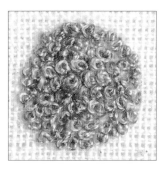 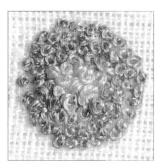 

Here, all the French knots have been worked, starting in the centre, in the same shade of yellow. Two threads were used and a single loop to form the knot.

A strand each of pale yellow and pale gold thread are used together for this flower centre. A cluster of three-loop French knots are worked in the centre surrounded with a few rounds of two-loop knots and finally rounds of one-loop knots to create a domed effect.

This flower centre has been worked in the same way as the one on the left, but using a lighter shade of yellow in the middle to emphasise the three-dimensional effect.

In this side view of a flower centre, the French knots have been worked into an oval shape, with darker shades used at the base and lighter ones just above the centre to give depth.

The centres of some flowers, such as some poppies and roses, are often surrounded with hair-like stamens. A simple but effective version can be made using the technique below.

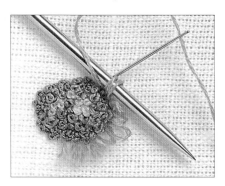  

1. Form loops around the outside of the flower centre, working the loops over a large second needle to control their size. Always take the needle back down at a slight angle to where it came up.

2. Work all the loops, then snip through the tops of the loops with small, sharp scissors and trim them to the correct length.

The completed flower centre. Use different coloured threads for different flowers.

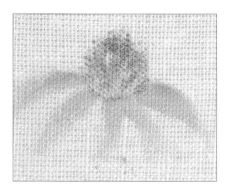 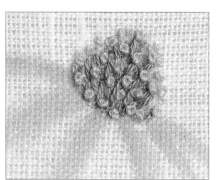

This domed flower centre, viewed from the side, was created by first embroidering a random number of green straight stitches, worked from the bottom up, over a painted background, then working yellow French knots over the top.

Some flower have a dense cluster of stamens that stand proud of the petals. Some can be worked directly into the flower centre, but others need to be made separately and then attached. Vary the number of strands you use to make different-sized stamens.

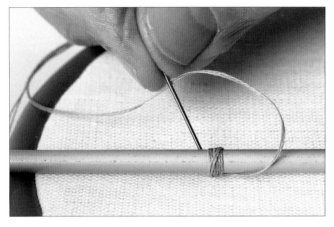

Tip

Waxing or soaping the thread before you start working can help the stamens stand more erect. It will hold the threads together as you work and form better stamens. See page 39.

1. Work a series of loops over a knitting needle or similar using two strands of embroidery thread. Alter the angle of the knitting needle slightly as you work to avoid the loops lying in a straight line. Never go through the same hole in the fabric twice.

2. Carefully remove the knitting needle and cut through the tops of the loops.

3. Separate and position the stamens using the point of a needle. Trim them if necessary.

Space is often limited in, for example, the centre of a trumpet-shaped flower. In this case it is easier to work longer loops of prepared (waxed or soaped) thread over the eye-end of a large needle and then trim to the length required. This method of working the stamens also prevents them from being accidentally pulled out from the front of the fabric.

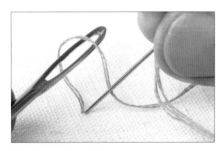

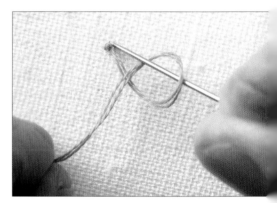

1. Knot the thread, bring the needle up through the fabric and take it back down in almost the same position.

2. Form a loop on the surface of the fabric over the eye-end of the needle.

3. Working on the back of the fabric, and without pulling the loop at the front through, wrap the thread around the needle once and place the point of the needle into the fabric close to where it comes through.

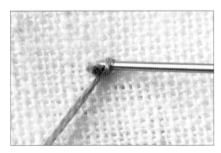

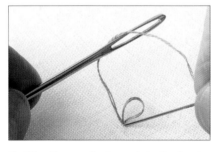

4. Hold the needle in place and pull the knot tight around the end of the needle, close to the fabric.

5. Take the needle through to the front of the fabric and form the next loop.

6. Continue making as many loops as you need, knotting each one individually on the back of the fabric. Cut through the tops of the loops, then trim and position the stamens as before.

A number of flowers, for example Aquilegia and Prunus, have a smaller group of individual stamens in the centre, with a clearly defined anther at the tip of the filament. These are worked on a piece of fabric secured in a hoop. They are then cut and attached in the centre of the flower.

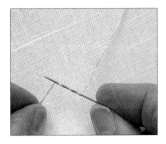

1. Bring the thread through to the front of the fabric and wind it around the needle several times, approximately 5cm (2in) from the base of the thread.

2. Grasp the wound thread on the needle between your finger and thumb.

3. Pull the needle through, retaining your hold on the wound thread until it is completely pulled through.

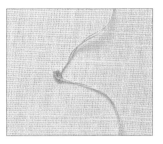

4. Form the knot, then create several more knots along the length of the thread, approximately 10cm (4in) apart.

5. Rub moist soap or beeswax along the length of the thread to hold the strands together and keep the stamens erect when in place.

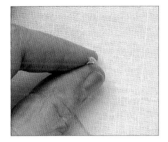

6. Cut the thread halfway between each knot ('anther') to leave a 5cm (2in) tail either side. Roll the two tails together to form the stalk ('filament'). The soap will help hold them together.

7. Thread the ends of two stamens at a time into a needle and take the ends only through the flower centre. Check the length of the stamens at the front, then oversew the ends at the back with a fabric-coloured thread to secure.

Tip

If you are using a number of threads, for example to create a stamen or a stem, it is a good idea to wax them. The wax holds the threads of a stem together, and makes the stamens stand up. Alternatively, use a block of dry soap.

Wax the threads by drawing them firmly across the edge of a beeswax block.

A length of unwaxed threads.

The same threads, after they have been waxed.

Pistils are larger and thicker than stamens and are found in the centre of some flowers, surrounded by the stamens. Make different-sized pistils by varying the number and length of strands of thread used. For a large pistil, like that found in the centre of a lily, use a thick cotton thread.

1. Make a knot in the centre of a length of thread, fold the thread in half at the knot, then make a series of knots along the length of the double thread, sliding each one up to meet the one above as you go along so there are no gaps in between.

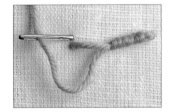

2. Attach the pistil to your embroidery by threading each tail into a needle and taking them through to the back of the work, as close to each other as possible. Knot the threads together to secure the stitch.

The completed pistil.

Poppy centres

Poppy centres vary in size, and consist of a large, central stigma surrounded by stamens. To create the 'stigmatic disc', as it is called, start with a disc made from interfacing (this one is 1.25cm (½in) in diameter), a piece of wadding the same size, and a green silk disc 3cm (1½in) in diameter, that is approximately two-and-a-half times the width of the interfacing disc. Do not anchor the thread, but stitch a narrow hem around the edge of the silk using tiny running stitches and a toning thread. Do not fasten off the thread.

1. With the hem uppermost, place the interfacing and then the wadding in the centre of the silk disk. Take another thread through the centre of both discs and the silk, then work a tiny stitch back through to secure all three layers together. Leave a long tail thread.

2. Place a finger firmly on top of the disks and pull the threads at both ends of the running stitches to gather the silk around the filling.

3. Secure the two threads by tying them together in a double knot and trimming off the ends. Use a pale green thread to work tiny running stitches just underneath the rim of the silk disk.

4. Pull the thread to gather the fabric neatly around under the edge of the silk disk and anchor it off.

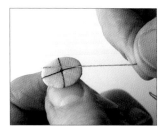

5. Using the tail thread from the centre stitch, work two stitches across the centre of the disk to form a cross, taking each end of the stitches through the edge of the disk and the wadding to hold them securely.

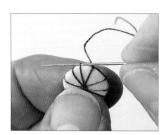

6. Work two more stitches across to segment the disk and work a small stitch over them in the centre to secure them. Finally, weave the thread around the edge of the disk, wrapping it once around the base of each stitch, to create the rim.

Stems

Having carefully embroidered a flower or leaf, it is important to make the stem as life-like as possible. Each group of flowers has its own type of stem, for example some are strong and straight, others are thin and flexible, while others bend under the weight of the flower itself. Colour and texture also play an important part. Vary the width of a stem by using different numbers of threads, and alter the tone by combining different coloured strands to form a single stem thread. Stems can be couched in place to curve them or to create a kink, and it is important that the couching stitches do not show. Work them at an angle at intervals along the stem using fairly long stitches and as few stitches as possible, using a strand of toning thread. Some stems have thorns, and these can also be used to secure the stem in position.

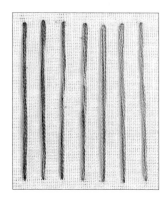

Varying the colour

The stems to the left show the different shades of green that can be achieved simply by varying the colours of the threads used. I have used six strands and gradually increased the number of strands in the lighter tone and decreased the number of darker ones as you go from left to right.

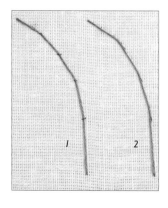

Couching stems

The couching stitches should be made as invisible as possible. The stitches are approximately 0.5cm (¼in) long and worked at the same angle as the twist of the stem thread (stem 2 on the left). They should not be worked straight across the stem, as this makes them more visible (stem 1). You may need to practice a few stitches first.

Finishing off

When your embroidery is complete, hold it up to the light and check for stray threads or ribbon on the back, which will show through on the front when the embroidery is mounted and framed, and either cut them off or, if necessary, sew them in. If any petals or leaves have become flattened or misshapen, moisten them, or leave the embroidery for a while in a steamy atmosphere such as a bathroom, then use the eye-end of a second needle to lift and reposition them, as shown in the steps below.

1. Lift (using the eye-end of a large needle) and moisten any petals that have become flattened or misshapen.

2. Re-form the hollow at the base of the petal using a cotton bud.

3. If you wish, use a hairdryer to speed up the drying time while supporting the petal.

4. Petals can be supported with a small pad of wadding placed under the petal, if necessary.

Where petals have been built up in layers, start with the petals worked first and lift each petal in turn using the eye-end of a needle.

The flowers

Aquilegia, page 44

Aster, page 46

Buddleia, page 48

Chrysanthemum, page 50

Crambe, page 54

Delphinium, page 56

Digitalis, page 58

Erica, page 60

Euphorbia, page 62

Fuchsia, page 64

Galanthus, page 68

Hydrangea, page 70

Iris, page 72

Jasminum, page 74

Kniphofia, page 76

Lathyrus, page 78

42

Lavandula, page 80

Monarda, page 82

Narcissus, page 86

Orchid, page 90

Papaver, page 94

Pelargonium, page 98

Prunus, page 100

Rosa, page 102

Scabiosa, page 106

Tropaeolum, page 108

Ursinnia, page 112

Viola, page 114

Wisteria, page 116

Xeranthemum, page 120

Yucca, page 122

Zantedeschia, page 124

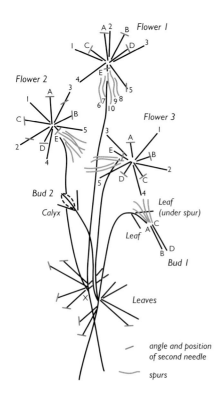

A 2   B   *Flower 1*
I   C   D   3
E
Flower 2
4
3
A
I
C   B
2   E   5
D
4
  7 9 8
6 10
5
Flower 3
3   A   I
E
B
D   C   2
5   4
Bud 2
Calyx
Leaf (under spur)
Leaf   A   C
B   D
Bud 1
X
Leaves

⟋   angle and position of second needle

⌣   spurs

The template, half actual size; enlarge to 200 per cent. Begin by marking each end of petals 1–5 of flowers 1, 2 and 3, buds 1 and 2, and the main leaves. Lift the template and lightly draw in the first 0.5cm (¼in) of each connecting line, starting at the base. Replace the template and mark in petals A–D of flowers 1, 2 and 3, and the leaves at the base of bud 1. Lift the template and draw these in, then finally replace the template and mark each end of the spurs in the same way.

2.5m (98¾in) 7mm Yellow (No. 15)

1.25m (49¼in) 4mm Yellow (No. 15)

0.67m (26½in) 7mm Just Green (No. 31)

0.5m (19¾in) 4mm Just Green (No. 31)

30 x 40cm (11¾ x 15¾in) linen/cotton fabric; stranded threads in Green (No. 216), Just Green (No. 859), Pale Yellow (No. 292) and a white thread to match the background fabric; silk paints in poppy red, magenta, navy blue and primary yellow; fabric paints in cardinal red, cobalt blue and buttercup yellow.

Aquilegia

These delicate, bell-shaped flowers, also known as granny's bonnets, are found in gardens and meadows across much of the northern hemisphere. A promiscuous perennial, it seeds freely to produce a range and combination of colours that are second to none.

It was a very grey day when I chose this explosion of colour, like rays of sunshine, to embroider. The form of the flower is, in effect, a trumpet within a trumpet and is worked in two colours, with each petal placed and shaped, and then anchored off before starting the next.

Painting the ribbon

1 Using silk paint, mix red with a touch of magenta and dilute it with a little water to make a soft orange. Moisten a 1m (39½in) length of 7mm Yellow ribbon with water and paint the entire length. Leave to dry. Cut a 20cm (7¾in) length of the same ribbon, moisten it and paint 3cm (1¼in) at each end. Using the same mix, moisten the 4mm Yellow ribbon and paint it randomly to produce a mottled effect (see page 15). Leave to dry. Mix blue and yellow silk paint to make two shades of green, moisten both the 4mm and 7mm green ribbons and paint them randomly. Leave to dry. Press all the ribbons.

Flower 1

Note: shape and tilt every petal using a second needle; anchor the ribbon off before starting the next petal.

2 Anchor a length of 7mm dyed orange ribbon at the base of petal 1 and work a reverse centre ribbon stitch at the tip. Anchor off. Work petals 2 and 3 in the same way.

3 Cut a length of 7mm undyed yellow ribbon, fold one end in half lengthwise and thread this end into a needle (see page 22). Take it through the fabric at the base of petal A. Work a straight stitch at the tip, using a second needle to lift the petal just above the orange petals underneath, creating a hollow at the base and a full and rounded tip. Work petals B to D in the same way, taking C and D through the edge of the orange petal underneath.

4 Work petals 4 and 5 in the same way as petals 1 to 3 in step 2.

5 Work spurs 6 to 9 in order. For each one, thread a length of 4mm dyed orange ribbon into a needle and knot one end. Bring it up at the tip of the spur. Moisten your thumb and forefinger and roll the ribbon at the knotted end to form a coil about 2cm (¾in) long. Work a twisted straight stitch, as described on page 28. Fasten off.

6 Take the 20cm (7¾in) length of 7mm ribbon painted only at the ends and cut it in half. Tie a knot at the painted end of one half, then roll the

Spurs

Flower 1

Flower 2

Flower 3

ribbon and bring it up through the fabric at the tip of spur 10, as in step 5. Lay the ribbon flat over the centre of the flower, then curve it back towards the tip of the spur over the eye-end of a second needle held just above the flower centre to create a loop. Work a centre ribbon stitch at E, pulling the ribbon through carefully to create the lower yellow petal at the front. Use a single strand of toning thread to work a tiny stitch on the wrong side of the fabric to hold the curve of the spur in place.

7 Make the stamens following the method described on page 39. Mix together a little red, blue and yellow fabric paint to make a browny-orange. Hold the stamens up from the petals using tweezers and lightly touch the knots with paint using a fine paintbrush.

8 Make a soft orange by mixing red, magenta and yellow silk paint with a little water. Supporting one of the yellow petals with a needle, moisten it from the base with water and shade it lightly with the soft orange mix. Paint the remaining yellow petals in the same way.

Flowers 2 and 3

9 Flower 2 is made in the same way as flower 1, only do not take the needle through the edges of the orange petals underneath when forming petals C and D.

Flower 3 differs from flower 1 in that there are only four spurs, petal E is worked as petal C, but note the position of the second needle.

Bud 1

10 Using 7mm dyed orange ribbon, work straight stitches from A to B and C to D, each time pulling the ribbon gently away from the petal to elongate the stitch (see page 27). Next work the two leaves either side of the stem as centre ribbon stitches with 4mm dyed green ribbon on the right and left sides of the bud. Finally, work the four spurs using 4mm dyed orange ribbon as before.

Bud 2

11 Using 7mm dyed orange ribbon, work a pad stitch with a straight stitch over the top (see page 28). For the calyx, use 4mm dyed green ribbon to work a left and a right ribbon stitch on the left and right sides of the bud respectively.

Leaves and stems

12 Using 7mm dyed green ribbon, work each leaf from the base to the tip with a single straight stitch. Note the angle of the second needle.

Note: when working the stems, use the eye-end of the needle where necessary to pass the threads behind a petal or leaf and then proceed as normal.

13 Make up a stem thread using two strands each of Green and Just Green threads. Thread it into a needle and knot one end. Start the first stem behind the spurs of flower 1 (see template) and work a straight stitch to the base of the

stem. Bring the needle up to the right of the thread at X and take it down through the fabric behind the spurs of flower 2. Use a strand of toning thread to couch the stems in place. Anchor off all the threads. Work a stem from behind the spurs to the base of flower 3, couch it in place and secure the threads as before. Now use three threads only to complete the stems to buds 1 and 2.

Aster

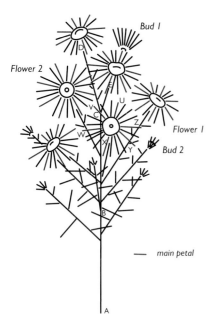

Bud 1

Flower 2

Flower 1

Bud 2

— main petal

The template, half actual size; enlarge to 200 per cent. Mark points A, B, C, D and E, and the base and tip of each side stem. When you have worked the stems, replace the template and mark each end of the main petals (shown in pink). Lightly draw in the flower centres only (not the lines connecting the ends of the petals).

5m (197½in) 2mm Deep Pink (No. 128)

1.75m (69in) 2mm Moss (No. 20)

1m (39½in) 4mm Moss (No. 20)

30 x 33cm (11¾ x 13in) linen/cotton fabric; stranded threads in Donkey (No. 393), Deep Moss (No. 268), Just Green (No. 859), Pale Yellow (No. 292), Yellow (No. 305) and a white thread to match the background fabric; silk paints in magenta, navy blue and primary yellow.

Clusters of these brightly coloured daisy-like flowers, usually with a yellow centre and up to 7.5cm (3in) across, burst into bloom at the end of summer and, depending on the weather, can continue well into winter. Also known as Michaelmas daisies, they vary greatly in height and may be grown in almost all garden situations, from rock gardens to borders.

Most of the petals are straight stitches, though a few are worked in ribbon stitch to give a sense of movement to those petals that often appear to sit slightly untidily round the centre. All the petals sit up from the fabric; in the oval flowers, the longer petals at the front are raised more than the shorter ones across the back to create form. Embroidered in one shade of deep pink, the base of each petal is then highlighted with magenta silk paint before working the French knot centres.

46

Stems

1 Make up a stem thread of six strands of Deep Moss and three strands of Donkey, thread it into a needle and knot one end. Moisten a small piece of soap and rub it along the thread from the knot end. Bring the needle up at A and secure the stem thread at B using two small stitches worked with a single strand of Deep Moss thread and a fine needle. Leave two Deep Moss and one Donkey strand to one side and secure the remaining six threads at C as before.

2 Divide the strands equally and take the resulting two threads through at D and E. Fasten off all the threads except the strands left at B. Use these to work the side stem from B and fasten off.

3 Using three strands as in step 2, work the remaining stems.

Flowers

4 Thread a length of 2mm Deep Pink ribbon into a size 24 needle and knot one end. Bring the needle up at the base of petal U of flower 1 and work a straight stitch at the tip. Work the remaining marked petals (V to Z) in order.

5 Referring to the picture and the template, work the rest of the petals of flower 1 in order going anti-clockwise around the centre of the flower. Fasten off.

6 Work the remaining five flowers and the petals of buds 1 and 2.

Painting the flowers

Note: use the eye-end of a needle to lift the petals up from the surface of the fabric to paint them and to reposition them after painting while they are still moist.

7 Using clean water and a fine paintbrush, moisten about two-thirds of each petal of flower 1 from the base to the tip. Using undiluted magenta silk paint, just touch the base of each petal with paint and allow the colour to fade gradually to about half way along.

8 Paint the rest of the flowers and leave to dry.

Flower centres

9 Work a cluster of three two-loop French knots in the centres of flowers 1 and 2 using a thread made up of one Pale Yellow and two Just Green strands. Fasten off after working each flower.

10 Make up a thread of two Pale Yellow strands and one Yellow and work one-loop French knots tightly around the centre ones of flowers 1 and 2 to not quite fill the flower centre and fasten off.

11 Use two Yellow strands and one Pale Yellow to work one-loop French knots around those just worked to complete the centres of flowers 1 and 2.

12 Referring to the template and to the picture, work a line of three two-loop French knots, as in step 9, for the remaining flowers, then complete them following steps 10 and 11.

Calyxes and leaves

13 Using 2mm Moss ribbon, work the two outer ribbon stitches of bud 1 then the three inner stitches. Fasten off. Work four ribbon stitches for the calyx of bud 2 followed by the two small leaves below it and fasten off.

14 Work the three green buds and the pair of small leaves below them in the same way.

15 Using the same ribbon, refer to the picture and work small leaves at random on the top parts of the stems. Use the 4mm Moss ribbon to work the remaining, larger leaves.

Painting the flower centres

16 Mix yellow and blue silk paint to make pale green then add a touch of red to make a soft brown. Dilute the mix to make a very pale honey shade and test it on a piece of white paper. Use a fine paintbrush to lightly shade the knots in the centre of each flower.

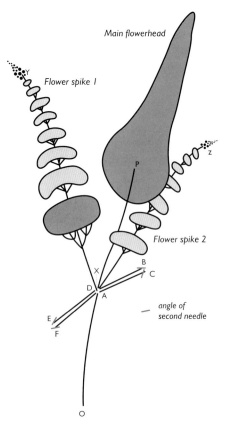

Main flowerhead

Flower spike 1

Flower spike 2

angle of second needle

The template, half actual size; enlarge to 200 per cent. Transfer the design to the linen/cotton fabric by marking with a dotted line the outlines of the main flowerhead and the flower shapes on spikes 1 and 2; the four stitches for the leaves (A-B, A-C, D-E and D-F), the main stem (O-X-P) and the two side stems (X-Y and X-Z).

You will also need to make a second full-size copy of the template and cut out the shapes for the main flowerhead and the lower part of spike 1 (shaded darker on the template).

12m (474in) 4mm Just Lilac (No. 83)

0.33m (13in) 7mm Cream (No. 156)

40 x 30cm (15¾ x 11¾in) linen/cotton fabric; 5 x 10cm (2 x 4in) wadding; 25 x 25cm (9¾ x 9¾in) white silk habitai; stranded threads in Just Green (No. 859), Soft Apple Green (No. 264), Sand (No. 854), Pale Yellow (No. 292) and a white thread to match the background fabric; silk paints in poppy red, magenta, navy blue and primary yellow; fabric paints in cardinal red, cobalt blue and buttercup yellow.

Buddleia

Found growing wild in many parts of the world, the butterfly bush, as this shrub is often called, has small, fragrant flowers that grow in large, tightly packed, mostly cone-shaped panicles. It is attractive to butterflies and a favourite of gardeners.

One shade of ribbon has been cut and dyed three different tones of lilac and then used to stitch the tiny flowers on to a piece of silk habitai. This was then attached over a padded base to create a raised embroidery.

Transferring the design to the silk and cutting out the wadding

1 Place the silk habitai in a hoop, pin on the two flower shapes (making sure they are at least 5cm (2in) apart), then make pencil dots around the outside of each one. Remove the cut-out paper shapes, pin them to the wadding and cut them out.

Painting the ribbon and the silk

2 Cut the 4mm Just Lilac ribbon into three 4m (158in) lengths. Mix a little blue and magenta silk paint and dilute it to make a very pale lilac. Moisten one length of ribbon and paint it randomly to create a mottled effect (see page 15). Leave to dry. Make the paint a little deeper in tone and repeat with another length, then make the colour a little deeper still and repeat for the last length. Leave to dry then press all the ribbons. Using a pencil, mark one end of each length L (light), M (medium) or D (dark) to identify the ribbons.

3 Using silk paints, make two shades of green using blue, yellow and a spot of red. Dye the 7mm Cream randomly, as in step 2.

4 Use the same mixes of green to paint the silk. Put in the part of the stem lying within the main flowerhead using a fine brush, then add some small spots of green either side. Mix some blue and magenta silk paint to make purple, dilute it a little, then apply the paint to both shapes by lightly touching the fabric with the tip of the paintbrush and allowing the paint to spread naturally. Press the silk when dry.

Painting the linen/cotton fabric

5 Mix a little blue fabric paint with magenta silk paint to make purple, dilute it a little, then very lightly dab paint in the flower sections using a clean, dry, stiff brush (see page 19). Make a green mix using a spot of blue silk paint and yellow fabric paint, and use the point of a fine brush to paint the buds at the top of spikes 1 and 2. Allow the paint to dry, and press.

Embroidering the flowers on the silk habitai

6 Each flower is 6 to 7mm (¼in) across and consists of four petals worked as straight stitches from the tip to the centre of the flower. Use the eye-end of a second needle to pull the ribbon over. Leave this needle in place to retain the shape of the petal while you bring the ribbon up at the tip of the next one, then remove it and work the remaining petals.

7 Starting with the 4mm deep purple ribbon, work the darkest flowers along the lower edge and up the right side of the main flowerhead (refer to the picture on page 49). Work the mid-tone flowers through the centre, and finish with the lightest flowers on the left side. Arrange the flowers randomly, placing the first petal of

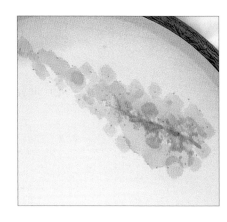

each successive flower in between the petals of the preceding one to avoid any gaps in your work. Work the lower section of spike 1 in the same way.

Attaching the main flowerhead to the fabric

8 Place the wadding for the main flowerhead on the linen/cotton fabric and hold it in position with two or three tacking stitches.

9 Cut out the main flowerhead from the silk habitai, cutting it 1.5cm (¾in) larger all the way round, and carefully pin it over the wadding. Working a small section at a time, fold the edges underneath, secure with pins, and use a toning thread to slip stitch the flowerhead in place. Take care not to compress the wadding too tightly.

10 Work some full and some half flowers over the sides of the padded area to give a slightly uneven edge. Finish the tip of the flowerhead with one-loop French knots, making them a little tighter as you approach the top.

Completing the main flowerhead

11 For the main stem, thread a needle with four strands each of Soft Apple Green and Sand thread, knot one end and wax the thread. Bring the thread up at O, pass it behind the flowers, and take it back down through the wadding at P. Fasten off.

12 Using a strand each of Soft Apple Green and Pale Yellow thread, work a one-loop French knot into the centre of each flower and half flower. Pull the knots down tighter in the flowers near the edge of the flowerhead to accentuate the domed effect.

13 Using a strand each of both green threads, work some short straight stitches at different angles in any spaces between the flowers to suggest stems.

Flower spike 1

14 Make a stem thread using two strands each of Soft Apple Green and Sand. Bring it up at X and down at Y. Fasten off.

15 Cut out the lower part of the spike from the silk and attach it to the linen/cotton fabric, as for the main flowerhead (see step 9). Follow step 10 to complete this part of the flowerhead.

16 Using a strand each of Soft Apple Green and Sand thread, work the small, straight stitch stems going from the main stem into the base of each section of the flowerhead, as marked on the template.

17 Using each of the three 4mm dyed purple ribbons to shade the flowerhead, work one-loop French knots, with looser ones in the centre, in the painted areas of the spike. Allow some of the painted background to show through for added depth.

Flower spike 2

18 Using the same methods as in steps 16 and 17 above, sew the stem from X to Z, and the smaller stems at the bases of the flower sections, as marked on the template. Fill the flower sections with French knots worked in the dyed dark purple ribbon.

Leaves

19 Using 7mm dyed green ribbon, bring the needle up at A and work a straight stitch at B, then work a left ribbon stitch from A to C. Anchor off. Anchor the end at D and work a left ribbon stitch to E and a right ribbon stitch from D to F. Anchor off.

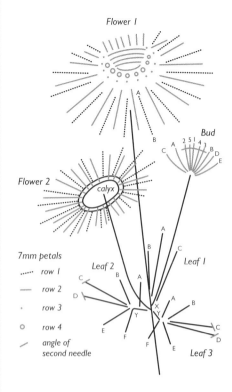

Flower 1

Bud

Flower 2

calyx

7mm petals

..... row 1

— row 2

· row 3

○ row 4

╱ angle of second needle

Leaf 2

Leaf 1

Leaf 3

Chrysanthemum

Flowering from mid-summer well into the winter, this flower brings back many childhood memories for me. Every Christmas Eve my father presented my mother with a large bunch of beautiful blooms that were always displayed in a large stone jug, and their distinct earthy perfume filled the air – Christmas had come at last. There are so many varieties: stems with a single flower and sprays of many flowers; flowers consisting of one row of petals and balls of exquisitely formed petals, and others with long spidery petals that twist and curl. With their strong, often woody stems and broad range of colours that includes white, yellow, bronze, rust, pink and purple, chrysanthemums are a favourite of both the flower arranger and the gardener.

I have worked this flower with bright pink ribbon and used silk paint to lightly shade the petals and highlight the shape. The ribbon is lifted over the eye-end of a second needle to position and shape each petal then, when stitched, the point of a needle is used to lift the tip of the petal so that it sits just above the one below.

Mixing the paint

1 Mix magenta, yellow and a little blue silk paint to the required shade (test on a small piece of ribbon). Make about a tablespoonful of this colour and seal it in the jar – this is the basic mix for the flowers.

Painting the ribbons for the leaves and the silk habitai

2 Mix together some blue and yellow silk paint on a tile to make a blue-green. Moisten the 7mm Just Green ribbon with clean water, then dye the ribbon randomly to create a mottled effect (see page 15). Dry the ribbon and press.

3 Use the same blue-green mix to dye the silk habitai.

Flower 1

Note: after each 7mm petal is worked, anchor off and then cut the ribbon before working the next petal. (Ribbon taken across at the back of the work will cause problems when stitching, and in most cases destroy or at least distort those petals already worked.)

4 Start with row 1 (14 petals) and anchor a length of 7mm Bright Pink ribbon at A. Work a reverse centre ribbon stitch at B. Work the two

petals either side of petal A-B in the same way, then continue working alternately from side to side until row 1 is complete. This pattern of working ensures the petals sit evenly around the flower.

5 Put a little of the base paint (see step 1) on to a tile. Use the eye-end of a needle to lift the first petal (A-B) and use a fine paintbrush to moisten it from its base to just short of the tip with clean water. Paint the petal using the basic mix, applying it at the base and allowing it to spread naturally towards the tip (because the tip is dry, it should not seep into the background fabric). Paint the remaining petals in the same way and leave to dry.

The template, half actual size; enlarge to 200 per cent. Begin by marking both ends of each petal in row 1 of flower 1. Lift the template and draw in the connecting lines. Repeat for row 2, then mark the dots in rows 3 and 4 (each dot represents a petal), the seven outer petals at the back of the flower (shown as seven vertical lines) and the five curved rows of petal lines in the middle. Re-pin the template and repeat for rows 1 and 2 of flower 2 and the petals of the bud. Mark the base of the main stem and the point where it intersects the two other stems. Finally, mark each end of the leaves and draw in the connecting lines of the two long leaves only.

5m (197½in) 7mm Bright Pink (No. 25)

2m (79in) 4mm Bright Pink (No. 25)

1.5m (59¼in) 4mm Apricot (No. 167)

0.75m (29½in) 4mm Soft Green (No. 33)

1.5m (59¼in) 7mm Just Green (No. 31)

33 x 33cm (13 x 13in) linen/cotton fabric; 3 x 3cm (1¼in) wadding; 5 x 5cm (2 x 2in) white silk habitai; stranded threads in Soft Brown (No. 904), Donkey (No. 393), Deep Moss (No. 268), Sand (No. 854) and a white thread to match the background fabric; silk paints in magenta, navy blue and primary yellow; small screw-top jar.

6 The 13 petals in row 2 are folded reverse ribbon stitches, which have more slender tips (see page 31). Work from the centre of the row outwards, and use the same ribbon as before. This time, lift the ribbon slightly higher to sit over row 1, and before anchoring off use the point of a needle to lift the tip of the petal a fraction on the right side (do this every time a petal sits over another petal or leaf). Paint the petals to complete row 2.

7 Row 3 (12 petals) is worked as row 2, but making the stitches a little shorter and lifting them over the previous row. The dots mark the base of each petal. Do not paint these petals yet.

8 Change to the 4mm Bright Pink ribbon and work the seven vertical centre ribbon stitch petals at the back of the flower. Work from left to right, to connect with each end of row 1. Paint these petals, and those in row 3.

9 Using 4mm Apricot ribbon, work a row of six centre ribbon stitches in a line across the base of the previous 4mm petals. Position them with the tips just below and between the petals of the row underneath. Use the line marked on the template as a guide. Mix a little of the basic colour with some magenta to make a deeper pink, and paint the centres of these petals, leaving the tips unpainted.

10 Work row 4 (8 petals) as row 3, with 7mm Bright Pink ribbon. Paint the petals with the basic mix.

11 Work another row of 4mm Apricot centre ribbon stitch petals, just below the previous row of 4mm petals. Fan the stitches out slightly, and paint them as in step 9. Work two more rows of these petals, stopping 5mm (¼in) from the base of row 4, and painting each row as you go. Use the curved lines marked on the template for guidance.

12 Still using the 4mm Apricot ribbon, note the direction of the curve and work a row of straight stitches. Bring the needle up just below the last row of 4mm petals, and take the needle down just below the tips of the petals in row 4. Use the eye-end of a second needle to control the ribbon, lifting the petals to make the centre of the flower fuller.

13 Using 7mm Bright Pink ribbon, work three or four randomly placed petals using folded reverse ribbon stitch, fanning them out slightly and lifting them over the 7mm petals underneath to give fullness to the flower. Paint these petals with the basic mix to complete flower 1.

Flower 2

14 The petals of this flower are all centre ribbon stitches worked with 7mm Bright Pink ribbon. Work row 1, paint the petals with the basic mix (see step 5), and then work row 2. Paint these petals in the same way.

15 Cut out a piece of wadding slightly larger than the calyx, then cut out a piece of green dyed silk not less than 1cm (½in) larger all round. Cover the wadding with the silk, tuck in the edges and place it in the centre of the flower. Slip stitch it in place with a coordinating thread. Mark the position of the stem with a pencil.

16 Thread a length of the 4mm Soft Green ribbon into a needle and bring it up through the fabric at the top of the stem. Work a series of centre ribbon stitches radiating outwards, taking the needle down through the bases of the petals. Leave a small hole at the centre.

Bud

17 Using 4mm Bright Pink ribbon, work centre ribbon stitches for petals 1 to 5 in order. Use a second needle to curve and shape the petals. Work stitches A to E in order, using right ribbon stitches at A and C, and left ribbon stitches at B, D and E. Paint these petals using the basic mix. Now work two rows of straight stitch petals

to fan out and fill the space between petals A and B, as indicated by the curved line on the template. Paint these petals in the same way.

18 The calyx, worked with 4mm Soft Green ribbon, consists of six centre ribbon stitches worked into the base of the petals and gently fanning outwards.

Here I have worked a variety of chrysanthemum buds (there always seem to be so many on a stem!). Small buds vary very little, but you can increase their size and add more petals for varying degrees of openness using the same ribbon as for the flowers.

Stems

19 The stems are made up of three strands each of Soft Brown, Donkey and Deep Moss, and one strand of Sand thread. Pull the strands singly then put them together to make a single thread and knot one end. Moisten a piece of dry soap and run it a few times from the knot end along the thread's length. Thread it into a large needle. Bring the needle up between the petals of flower 1 (see template) and take it back down at the base of the stem. Now bring the needle up at the base of flower 2's stem and take it down through the back of the flower. Fasten off. Finally work the stem for the bud and fasten off. Do not couch any parts of the stems yet – this should be done later, once the leaves are in place.

Leaves

20 For leaf 1, anchor a length of ribbon at the base of A and work a reverse centre ribbon stitch at A. Anchor off and repeat for B and C, placing them behind the stems.

21 For leaf 2, work a straight stitch at A and B, a left ribbon stitch at C, a right ribbon stitch at D and straight stitches at E and F. Bring the ribbon up at X and use a toning thread to work a tiny stitch over the ribbon at Y to hold it in position. Work a centre ribbon stitch at F to complete the leaf. Fasten off.

22 For leaf 3, work straight stitches at A, B and C, then a left ribbon stitch at D and a reverse centre ribbon stitch at E. Work F as for leaf 2. Fasten off.

23 To finish, couch the lower part of each side stem to produce a curve.

The first three chrysanthemum heads above are all worked in straight stitch using 4mm ribbon. The white single flower, number 1, has been lightly shaded in palest grey with a touch of yellow, and the yellow flower, number 2, has not been painted at all. Flower 3 uses three shades of red ribbon, starting with the darkest on the bottom, then the mid tone and the lightest shade on the top.

Flower 4 is a spider chrysanthemum worked with 2mm white ribbon that has been dyed randomly. The petals are twisted straight stitches (see page 28). The stitches are taken right into the centre of the flower, which has then been shaded a little deeper.

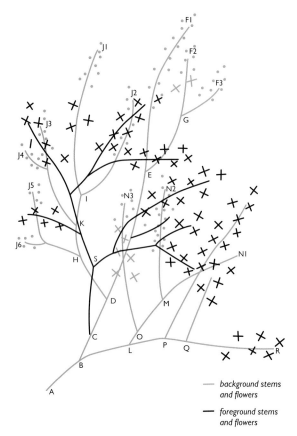

The template, half actual size; enlarge to 200 per cent. Transfer the stems marked in green on the template, remove the template and embroider these stems. Replace the template accurately, and transfer and work the remaining stems. Replace the template again to transfer the flowers marked in black. Lightly draw in the four petal lines of each flower. Finally, replace the template and mark the positions of the green flowers, including the dots.

You may prefer to mark the positions of only some of the flowers and work the remainder by eye.

— background stems and flowers

— foreground stems and flowers

5m (197½in) 2mm White (No. 03)

30 x 38cm (11¾ x 15in) linen/cotton fabric; stranded threads in Just Green (No. 859), Donkey (No. 393) and a white thread to match the background fabric; silk paint in navy blue; fabric paint in primary yellow.

Crambe

Crambe, or sea kale, with its sturdy stems and large, cabbage-like leaves to balance its mass at the base, makes a strong sculptural display. A huge, frothy mass of tiny white flowers, very like a large version of gypsophilia, is much loved and used frequently by florists. Often scented, the flowers each have four small petals that sit proudly on stems that cope well in windy areas such as the coast, as the name suggests.

Stems

1 Cut a 50cm (19¾in) length of each thread and make up a stem thread of four strands of green and two of brown. Thread it into a needle and knot one end. Moisten a piece of dry soap and lightly pull it along the thread from the knot end. Repeat when all of the soaped section of the stem thread has been worked into the embroidery.

2 Bring the thread up at A and couch it in place at B, C, D and along to E. Take one brown and one green strand through to the back and fasten both off. Couch two strands only to F1, fasten off, then couch the other two strands to G and F2. Fasten off. Cut another two of these strands to work G to F3. Fasten off.

3 Remembering to soap the thread when necessary, use three green strands and one brown to work the stem D-H-I. Divide the thread into two, each with two strands, and work to J1 and J2. Work H to J5 and J6, and K to J3 and J4 in the same way.

4 Using three brown strands and one green, thread a needle and bring the thread up at B. Couch at L, then couch two brown strands through to M and N1 and fasten off. Use the two remaining strands to work M-N2 and O-N3.

5 Couch two brown strands from L at P, Q and R, fasten off, then use two green threads for the stems starting at P and Q.

6 Transfer the remaining stems from the template. Work C to S using three green strands and one brown strand, then divide the thread as above to complete the stems.

Flowers

Note: work with a short length of 2mm ribbon (about 33cm (13in) long) as narrow ribbon deteriorates slightly as it is worked.

7 Transfer the foreground flowers from the template (shown in black). Thread a length of 2mm White ribbon into a size 24 needle and knot one end. Starting with a flower at the top of a main stem, make a hole in the centre of the flower using a large needle. Bring the needle up at the tip of a petal and take it down through the hole in the centre to form a straight stitch, using the eye-end of a second needle to pull the ribbon over. Keep this second needle in place and bring the ribbon up at the tip of the next petal, then remove it to shape the second petal as you take the ribbon down through the central hole. Form the remaining two petals in the same way.

8 Work the remaining foreground flowers in groups, from the top of each stem downwards; complete the flowers that are close to each other and fasten off before moving on to the next group. Do not take the ribbon across the back of the work.

9 Transfer the background flowers from the template. Those marked with a cross are worked in the same way as the foreground flowers; the remainder (marked on the template as a dot) are French knots. Work those at the tops of the stems as one-loop French knots and those slightly lower down as two-loop French knots.

Side stems

10 The tiny side stems connect each of the flowers to the main stems. Sew them by eye, referring to the picture above. Start at the top of a main stem each time and work downwards, using two strands of green thread for the main flowers and a single strand for the French knots. For each side stem, bring the needle up at the base of the flower and work a straight stitch to the main stem a little way below, taking the thread behind the flowers as needed. Do not pull the stitches too tight or take threads across the back of the work.

Painting the flowers

11 Mix the blue silk paint with yellow fabric paint to make a mid-green then use the point of a fine paintbrush to paint the very centre of each flower. Add just a touch of colour to the centre of each French knot.

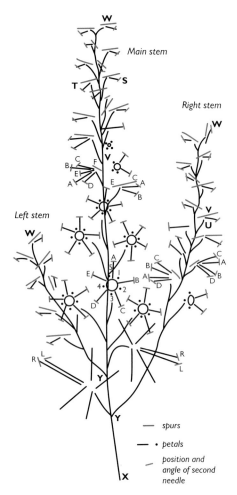

Main stem

Right stem

Left stem

— spurs

•— • petals

position and angle of second needle

The template, half actual size; enlarge to 200 per cent. Begin by transferring the stems only. Once you have embroidered the three main stems and the side stems (only those down to V on the main and right stems), replace the template accurately and transfer the rest of the design. Mark the leaves, fully and partly open flowers (each end of the petals and leaves, and the dots around the flower centres), then partly lift the template and lightly draw in the connecting lines and the centre circles. Replace the template and mark the positions of the buds, drawing in the petal lines only.

4m (158in) 7mm Soft Blue (No. 125)

2.5m (98¾in) 4mm Soft Blue (No. 125)

1m (39½in) 7mm Just Green (No. 31)

33 x 40cm (13 x 15¾in) linen/cotton fabric; stranded threads in Just Green (No. 859), Soft Apple Green (No. 264), Sand (No. 854), Black (No. 403), Pale Blue (No. 144) and a white thread to match the background fabric; silk paints in magenta, navy blue and primary yellow; fabric paint in primary yellow.

Delphinium

This spectacular, regal flower with its towering spires of closely packed, perfectly formed florets can be found growing wild in mountainous regions. What a sight this must be! The colours include white, blue, purple and pink, and now yellow and red. Without doubt, it is one of my favourite flowers.

This is a double flowered variety but you could work a single variety by simply not embroidering the upper petals. To work a flower spike like this, always start with the largest flowers at the base and make them progressively smaller towards the top.

Painting the ribbon

1 Mix together blue and a little magenta silk paint on a tile to make a blue with a hint of mauve, and dilute it with a little water. Moisten the 7mm Soft Blue ribbon with clean water then dye the ribbon randomly to create a mottled effect (see page 15). Leave to dry then press the ribbon.

2 Add a little water to the paint to make a slightly paler shade and dye the 4mm Soft Blue ribbon in the same way.

3 Mix blue and yellow silk paint to make a blue-green, dilute it a little then dye the Just Green ribbon as above.

Main stem

Note: avoid taking any threads across the back of the embroidery. Either fasten them off or run the threads directly behind the stem just worked.

4 Thread two strands of Soft Apple Green thread into a needle and knot one end. Bring the needle up at W, at the tip of the main central stem, and lay the thread down to X. Pin the thread to the fabric at the base of the stem to hold it in place.

5 Using two more strands of the same thread, work the top left-hand side stem. Bring the needle up at the tip of the side stem and pass it through to the back where it joins the main stem, couch the thread in position and fasten off. Work the next three side stems in the same way, fastening off as each one is worked.

6 Using a strand each of Soft Apple Green and Just Green thread, work the next side stem down from the top (S), but this time take the thread down to the base of the stem (X) instead of passing it through to the back, and place it under the pin. Repeat for the next side stem (T), bringing the number of strands in the main stem up to six. Take all the strands through to the back at X, couch the stem and the two side stems (S and T) into position and fasten off.

7 Use the same two strands of thread to work the remaining side stems down to V only (all the remaining side stems are worked after the flowers have been embroidered).

Right and left stems

8 Using two strands of Soft Apple Green thread, as before, work the right stem W-Y in the same way as the main stem, pinning it in place at Y. Work all of the side stems down to V. Work the next side stem on the right (U) using a strand of each green, but only take the Just Green strand down to Y. Take all three threads to the back of the fabric at Y, couch the stem in place and fasten off.

9 Using two strands of Pale Apple Green thread, work the left stem and each of its side stems. Couch in place as before.

Fully open flowers

Note: always work the petals in order around the centre of a flower; avoid taking the ribbon across the flower centre on the wrong side of the fabric as this will cause you to accidentally stitch through the ribbon. Anchor off after each flower is worked.

10 Begin with the large flower in the middle, at the bottom of the main stem. Anchor a length of 7mm dyed blue ribbon at the base of petal A. Using the eye-end of a second needle to control the ribbon and give fullness at the petal tip, work the petal as a straight stitch. Work petals B to E in the same way.

11 Work the inner petals (1 to 5) so that their loop edge lies just within those of the outer petals. Bring the needle up at 1 and form a petal

by folding the ribbon over the eye-end of a second needle. Lay the ribbon across the centre of the flower and work a centre ribbon stitch, taking the needle back through the ribbon just within the centre circle. Keep the second needle in the fold as the ribbon is pulled through to the back to complete the stitch. Bring the needle up again at 2, then remove the second needle and work petals 2 to 5 in order in the same way.

12 Thread a fine needle with two strands of black thread and knot one end. Bring the needle up through the centre of petal 1, 0.5cm (¼in) from its base, and take it down on the edge of the circle to form a tiny straight stitch. Repeat for petals 2 to 5.

13 Make a cluster of stamens in the centre of the flower using a strand each of Soft Apple Green and Sand thread (see page 38).

14 Work the remaining fully open flowers in the same way, using centre ribbon stitch for petals marked with a dot, and straight stitch for those marked with a line.

Partly open flowers

15 Work the petals of the four partly open flowers as straight stitches using 7mm dyed blue ribbon. Note carefully the angle of the second needle marked on the template, and work them in alphabetical order. Use 4mm dyed blue ribbon and work a straight stitch for the spurs.

Buds

16 Use 7mm dyed blue ribbon for the larger buds and 4mm ribbon for the smaller buds and all the spurs. Work each of the petals and spurs as straight stitches, shaping and curving them as shown on page 27 using a second needle. Place some of the buds under the stem.

Completing the stems

17 Using a strand each of Soft Apple Green and Just Green work the remaining side stems (see step 5). Couch the stems in position.

Leaves

18 Using 7mm dyed green ribbon, work the four lower leaves on each stem as centre ribbon stitches. For the main leaves use left and a right ribbon stitches (as indicated by L and R on the

template). Complete the stems as before (see step 15).

Painting

19 Add a green tinge to the base of each bud using a dilute pale green mix of blue and yellow silk paints.

20 Mix the green with some yellow fabric paint and use a fine brush to paint a few fine veins on each leaf and leave to dry. Mix a little blue and yellow silk paint to make a deeper green, then lightly shade each leaf. Leave to dry.

Digitalis

The tall, elegant foxglove stands proud and almost arrogant, with its delicate, tubular, bell-shaped flowers. They can be found growing wild in woodlands in many parts of the world and are a common sight in the woods where I live. The flowers, large enough to place a finger inside and loved by bees, are mostly shades of pink to mauve in the wild, but when cultivated can be found in many colours. I have used pale pink and deep pink ribbons for the petals, and painted on the spots before subtly shading each flower.

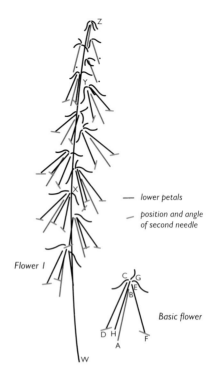

— lower petals

∕ position and angle of second needle

Flower I

Basic flower

The template, half actual size; enlarge to 200 per cent. Transfer the main stem and the petals marked in pink only. Lightly draw in the connecting lines. Replace the template and clearly mark each end of the two outer petals of each flower.

0.75m (29½in) 13mm Pink (No. 08)

0.5m (19¾in) 7mm Pink (No. 08)

2m (79in) 7mm Deep Pink (No. 128)

1.5m (59¼in) 4mm Moss (No. 20)

27 x 33cm (10¾ x 13in) linen/cotton fabric; stranded threads in Soft Apple Green (No. 264) and a white thread to match the background fabric; silk paints in magenta and navy blue; fabric paints in primary yellow, buttercup yellow and white.

Painting the stem thread

1 Mix some blue silk paint with a little of both yellow fabric paints to make a deep green. Cut a 66cm (26in) length of the green thread and roll it loosely around three fingers. Wet with clean water, then place the roll of thread on the paint and push paint into it with a small, stiff brush. Suspend to dry.

Stem

2 Cut the length of green dyed thread in half, pull ten strands in all from both lengths singly and reassemble them to make the stem thread. Knot one end, thread it into a needle and rub a piece of moist soap along most of the length from the knot end.

3 Bring the needle up at W and pull the thread between a large needle and your thumb to flatten it and make the stem wider at the base. Lay the stem thread in place, taking three strands through to the back at X, the same again at Y and the remaining four at Z. Make sure the stem thread retains its shape and re-soap as necessary. Fasten off all the threads.

4 Use a coloured thread to work temporary single straight stitches at intervals across the stem to hold it in place while working the flowers (this thread will be removed when the embroidery is finished).

Flowers

Note: when securing the ends of 7 and 13mm ribbons (see page 23), work two stitches across the width of the ribbon, concealed behind the petal about to be worked, to prevent it twisting on the right side. Anchor off each petal as it is worked.

5 Anchor the end of a length of 13mm Pink ribbon at A of flower 1. Work a centre ribbon stitch at B, using a cotton bud to pull the ribbon over and shape the tip of the petal.

6 Anchor a length of 7mm Deep Pink ribbon at C and work a left ribbon stitch at D. Note the angle of the second needle placed in the loop as the ribbon is pulled through to the back; tilt this needle so that the edge of the ribbon at the centre is lifted to start forming the tubular shape. Anchor the same ribbon at E and work a right ribbon stitch at F, then anchor the ribbon at G and work a centre ribbon stitch at H, lifting it to complete the curved tube shape at the base of the flower. Fasten off.

58

7 Work the next four flowers up the stem in the same way. Work the next four slightly smaller flowers in straight stitch with only two Deep Pink petals which meet at the centre. For the next three flowers, which are smaller still, use the 7mm Pink ribbon for the first stitch (shown in pink on the template) and work straight stitches over that using the Deep Pink ribbon. The topmost flower has a Pink straight stitch worked first then a Deep Pink one worked over it, allowing a hint of colour to show from the lower petal at one side.

Painting the flowers

Note: place the embroidery on a foam pad and use pins to hold the petals away from those being painted (see page 17). Paint one flower at a time, from the bottom of the stem upwards. Take care not to allow paint to seep into the background fabric.

8 Using white fabric paint and the point of a fine paintbrush, paint tiny dots at random on the lower pale pink petal of each flower and leave to dry. Mix a little blue and magenta silk paint and dilute it to make a pale mauve. Carefully moisten the visible part of the lower petal, from the rolled edge up to the base of the rolled tip of the pink top petals, then apply a little of the paint and allow it to fade out towards the tip. Leave to dry.

9 Mix the magenta and blue silk paint to a deeper tone than that of the Deep Pink ribbon and dilute it a little. Carefully moisten the Deep Pink petals from the base up to where the needle passed through the ribbon, then paint the top of each petal only and the side closest to the stem.

10 Paint the remaining flowers in the same way.

11 Mix a little more of the deep pink paint, making it a little deeper, and dilute it slightly. Without moistening the ribbon, repaint some of the petals down the side that are in deepest shade. When dry, use undiluted white fabric paint to paint a highlight on the domed area – the paint will fade gradually into the ribbon but will add a three-dimensional quality to the finished flower.

12 Mix a little white fabric paint with a little blue silk paint and a touch of magenta silk paint to make a browny mauve. Use the tip of a fine brush to place a tiny dot in the centre of some of the white dots on the pale pink ribbon. Leave to dry.

Leaves

13 Referring to the picture and the template, work the ribbon stitch leaves at random using the 4mm Moss ribbon, tucking some under the flower petals. Start with the small leaves at the top.

14 Mix a little primary yellow fabric paint with a touch of blue silk paint to make a deep green, and paint in some dark areas near the stem-end of each leaf using a fine brush. Leave to dry.

To finish

15 Remove the temporary stitches that were worked to hold the stem in place. Use the eye-end of a large needle placed in the roll of the petal tips to reposition and lift any petals that may have moved when being painted.

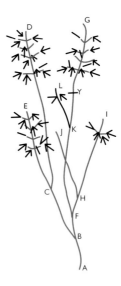

The template, half actual size; enlarge to 200 per cent. Transfer the design after you have painted the background. Mark the ends of the stems and the points where two stems cross. Work the stems, then replace the template and mark the centre petal only of the flowers with three petals; mark both petals of the two-petal flowers; and place a dot at the base of each single-petal flower.

Erica

Heather is a hardy, evergreen, ground-covering plant which, when in bloom, colours vast areas of both dry heathland and wet moorland. It has mostly green, needle-like leaves, but there are some with leaves that range from almost yellow to orange and red, and the tiny, bell-like flowers vary from white through every shade of pink to purple.

A piece of kitchen string, dyed and then untwisted, has been used for the woody stem. The background leaves are worked with embroidery thread with a few at the front worked in 2mm ribbon. The main bell-shaped flowers each have three petals: a straight stitch suggesting the back of the bell and a left and right ribbon stitch worked over the top to create the bell shape tilting forwards. Two-petalled flowers hang down and a single straight stitch is worked for partly open flowers or buds.

Painting the background

1 Mix yellow and blue silk paints to make two greens and dilute them to make them very pale (do not worry if the colours run into each other on the tile). Wet the fabric with clean water then lightly dab on the paint at random in the area to be embroidered. While it is drying, paint the string for the stem (step 2).

Painting the string

2 Mix yellow and blue to make a deep green and add a touch of red to make a deep grey-brown. Wet the string, remove any excess water with a paper towel then drop the string on to the paint. Use a stiff brush to work the paint into the string. While it is drying, paint the ribbon for the leaves (step 3).

2.5m (98¾in) 4mm White (No. 03)

1.5m (59¼in) 2mm Moss (No. 20)

26 x 30cm (10¼ x 11¾in) linen/cotton fabric; stranded threads in Deep Moss (No. 268), Moss (No. 266), Donkey (No. 393), Delph Blue (118) and a white thread to match the background fabric; silk paints in poppy red, navy blue and primary yellow; 20cm (7¾in) length of kitchen string.

Painting the ribbon for the leaves

3 Make a deep green, moisten the 2mm Moss ribbon and dye it randomly. Dry and press.

Stems

Note: to remove kinks and twists from the string, moisten it with water using a small, stiff paintbrush.

4 Cut a 15cm (6in) length of dyed string and untwist all but 4cm (1½in) of one end. Moisten the string with a little water to make it easier to shape, then place the untwisted end at A and use a pin through the back of the fabric to secure it in place at B. Take one strand to C, partly unravel it and couch the thickest part to D. Cut the end at an angle and use a toning thread to secure it with two or three stitches. Repeat for C-E with the thinner strand.

5 Now take the rest of the string at B to F, untwist it and couch one strand from F to G. Repeat step 4 for stem F-H and then H-I and H-J.

6 Use a thin strand of string for stem K-L and the small flower stems. Couch them in place.

Leaves

7 Make up a thread of two strands of Deep Moss and one of Moss,

thread it into a needle and knot one end. Referring to the picture and template, work a straight stitch for each of the three tiny leaves at the top of stem C-D, then work the small leaves in each angle between the main stem and the flower stem. Work groups of three leaves at intervals down the stem, positioning them as shown in the picture.

8 Work stems C-E and H-I in the same way, using the same thread. For stems H-J, K-L and K-G, use three strands of Deep Moss. Work stem K-G down to Y and fasten off.

Flowers

Note: the main flowers have three petals – a centre petal, worked as a straight stitch, with slightly shorter left and right ribbon stitches worked over the top to create a bell shape. Each main flower is between 5 and 7mm (about ¼in) long. A few flowers consist of just two ribbon stitches and there are four background flowers of only one ribbon stitch to create form.

Place the eye-end of a second needle in the loop of the ribbon stitch to create the lip of the petal, and to prevent the ribbon being pulled too tight and destroying the petal shape. To stop the flowers from being too big, the left and right ribbon stitches must be

worked either just on or just off the selvedge.

9 Thread a 33cm (13in) length of 4mm White ribbon into a size 18 needle, knot one end and bring the needle up at the base of a three-petal flower. Pulling the ribbon over the eye-end of a size 24 needle, work the centre petal (see note above). Keeping the second needle in place, bring the sewing needle up through the fabric just above the base of the first petal. Work the left-hand petal as a left ribbon stitch, removing the second needle and placing it in the loop to shape it. Repeat for the right-hand petal, which is worked as a right ribbon stitch. Leave the second needle in place.

10 Bring the needle up at the base of the next three-petal flower on the same stem, removing the second needle from the first flower only when you need it to

shape the centre petal. Complete the remaining three-petal flowers and then the two-petal flowers on the stem. Fasten off.

11 Work the flowers on the other stems in the same way.

Completing the leaves

12 Using the 2mm dyed green ribbon, work ribbon stitches to complete the remaining leaves, following the picture for guidance.

Flower centres

13 Thread a strand each of Delph Blue and Deep Moss thread into a fine needle and knot one end. Work a one-loop French knot into the centre petal of each three-petal flower, tucking it under the two top petals so that just a little of it shows.

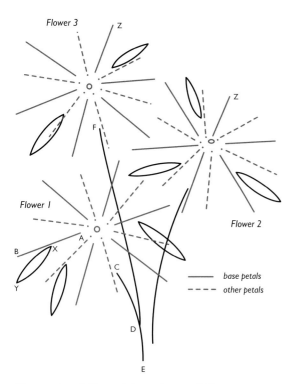

Flower 3

Flower 1

Flower 2

base petals
other petals

The template, half actual size; enlarge to 200 per cent. Mark each end of all the petals and leaves and the base of each stem. Remove the template and lightly draw in the connecting lines on the base petals only (shown as solid red lines on the template) and the large dot in the centre of each flower.

3m (118½in) 13mm Poppy Red (No. 02)

1m (39½in) 13mm Just Green (No. 31)

0.5m (19¾in) 4mm Just Green (No. 31)

0.5m (19¾in) 2mm Just Green (No. 31)

38 x 33cm (15 x 13in) linen/cotton fabric; stranded threads in Deep Moss (No. 268), Moss (No. 266), Soft Apple Green (No. 264), Yellow (No. 305) and a white thread to match the background fabric; silk paints in poppy red, navy blue and primary yellow; fabric paints in cobalt blue and buttercup yellow.

Euphorbia

Christmas simply would not be Christmas without the brilliant splash of red that a poinsettia provides. Also known as the Mexican flame leaf, it is usually deep red in colour, although it can also be a lighter red through to pink and even white.

What appear to be petals are in fact bracts, and these are worked after the leaves. I have used mainly 13mm ribbon worked in ribbon stitch, with some straight stitches to shape the leaves and petals.

Painting the ribbon for the leaves

1 Mix blue and yellow silk paints to make a bright green. Moisten the 13mm Just Green ribbon then paint it along its length with a large, stiff brush. Leave the ribbon to dry and press it.

Leaves

Note: fasten the ribbon off as each petal or leaf is worked.

2 Starting with flower 1, anchor one end of the 13mm dyed green ribbon at the base of one of the leaves (X) and work a centre ribbon stitch at Y. Fasten off and work the other two leaves.

3 Mix a deep green using blue and yellow fabric paint. Do not add water to the mix. Using the tip of a fine dry brush, carefully paint in the veins. Leave to dry.

4 Using silk paints, make another deep green. Lightly moisten a leaf with water, then paint it gently to suggest a shaded area under the petal yet to be worked. Avoid painting the very tip of the leaf to prevent paint seeping into the background fabric.

5 Paint the other two leaves of flower 1 and allow them to dry. Work the leaves of flowers 2 and 3 in the same way.

Flowers

6 Using 13mm red ribbon, fold one end in half lengthwise and thread this end into a large needle (see page 22). Beginning with flower 1, anchor one end of the ribbon at A (see page 23). Work the first petal (A–B) as a centre ribbon stitch with a slight lift. Fasten off, and work the remaining base petals (marked on the template as solid red lines) in order around the centre of the flower.

7 Change to the 4mm Just Green ribbon, bring the needle up at A and work a centre ribbon stitch, taking the needle down just outside the centre dot to leave a very small opening in the middle.

8 Now work the six other centre ribbon stitch petals, lifting each one at the centre to sit above those already worked. Use the 2mm Just Green ribbon to work the small centre ribbon stitches in the middle of the flower.

9 Work flowers 2 and 3 in the same way as flower 1, except that in each case petal Z is a straight stitch.

Painting the flower centres

10 Mix a spot of yellow and blue silk paint to make green. Without diluting it, paint the ends of the 2 and 4mm green stitches that are nearest the centre of the flower, then use red to paint the other ends, taking the paint up to the base of the petals. Allow to dry.

11 Use fabric paint to make a small amount of dark green. Do not dilute it. With a dry, fine brush, paint a thin central vein approximately 1.5cm (¾in) long from the base through the centre of each petal.

Stamens

12 Using two strands of Yellow thread and a size 24 needle, work 10 to 12 four-loop French knots (not too tight) in the centre of each flower and fasten off (see page 36). Using the eye-end of the needle, lift each knot from the surface of the fabric to create stamens.

Stems

13 Make up a stem thread using two strands of Deep Moss, four of Moss and one of Apple Green stranded thread. Knot one end and wax the thread to flatten it. Bring the thread up at C behind flower 1, take it down at D, up again at E and down at F, passing it behind flowers 1 and 3. Anchor off. Couch the stems in place with a toning thread. Work the stem of flower 2 using the same thread.

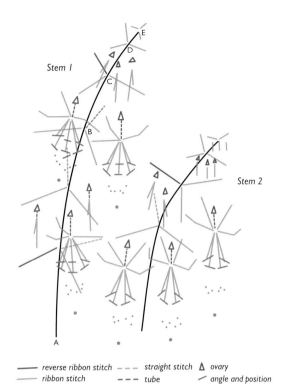

Stem 1

Stem 2

E
D
C
B
A

——— reverse ribbon stitch – – – straight stitch △ ovary
——— ribbon stitch - - - tube ⟋ angle and position
of second needle

The template, half actual size; enlarge to 200 per cent.
Transfer the design after you have painted the background.
First transfer the ends of the stems and leaves. Lifting half
of the template at a time, lightly draw in the connecting
lines, apart from the three small leaves at the top of stem 1.
Replace the template and mark the positions of the petals,
sepals and tubes, and each end of the buds. Draw in the
connecting lines of the petals and buds only.

1m (39½in) 13mm Just Green (No. 31)

0.5m (19¾in) 7mm Just Green (No. 31)

0.25m (9¾in) 4mm Just Green (No. 31)

1m (39½in) 7mm Purple (No. 177)

1m (39½in) 7mm Soft Poppy (No. 48)

0.5m (19¾in) 4mm Soft Poppy (No. 48)

1m (39½in) 7mm Pink (No. 08)

1m (39½in) 7mm Just Pink (No. 05)

0.33m (13in) 4mm Just Pink (No. 05)

0.5m (19¾in) 4mm Deep Green (No. 21)

0.25m (9¾in) 2mm Deep Green (No. 21)

Fuchsia

Fuchsias have charmed gardeners and flower lovers for hundreds
of years. With their sepals like arms and wings, delicately frilled
petal skirts and long, thin leg-like stamens, they are often called
the 'ballerina flower' as they dance gently in the slightest breeze.
The flowers range from miniature to large and showy, and come
in a range of vivid and dramatic colours. The endless names
of the different varieties allow the embroiderer to create the
perfect gift, perhaps Annabelle for a special friend of the same
name, or Love's Reward to celebrate a wedding or engagement,
to name but two.

Here I have painted a background of leaves then worked the
stems and leaves in ribbon stitch and straight stitch. The sepals
of the flowers are ribbon stitches, and I have used two different
methods of straight stitch for the purple and pink petals. Care
must be taken when stitching a petal through a leaf; each must
be lifted with the point of a needle to position.

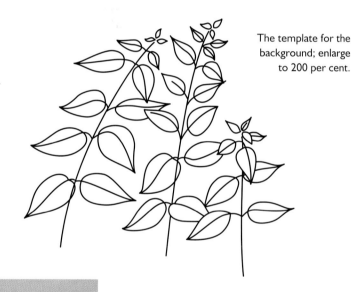

The template for the
background; enlarge
to 200 per cent.

Y
X
A
C E Z
H I Basic flower diagram.
D G F
B

32 x 32cm (12½ x 12½in) linen/cotton fabric;
stranded threads in Deep Moss (No. 268), Just Green
(No. 859), Sand (No. 854), Fuchsia Pink (No. 29), Pink
(No. 75), Deep Rose (No. 970), Maroon (No. 44) and
a white thread to match the background fabric; silk
paints in poppy red, raspberry, navy blue and primary
yellow; fabric paints in cardinal red, cobalt blue and
buttercup yellow.

Painting the background

Note: always use less paint on your brush than you think you need – it is easier to add more paint than to take it away.

1 Transfer the design for the background, lightly drawing in the main stems and the start of the central leaf veins. Using fabric paint, mix blue and yellow to make a pale green then add a touch of red to make it slightly brown. Dilute the mix a little to make it paler. Using a clean, dry, fine brush, lightly paint the left-hand stem from the base upwards, making it thinner towards the top.

2 Mix a dark green and, starting with the lower leaves, paint the vein lines from the stem towards the tip of each leaf.

Note: practise on a spare piece of fabric first.

Dilute the paint to make it slightly paler then use a stiff, straight-edged brush to lightly paint on the leaf surfaces. Start at the vein and use curved brushstrokes, lifting the brush at the edges of the leaves to make them lighter (see page 19).

3 Add a touch of red to the mix and very lightly paint in some tiny buds at the top of the stem. Leave to dry.

4 Paint the other two stems in the same way, adding a little more red to the mix for the centre stem to make a brown-green.

Painting the ribbons

5 Using silk paint, mix yellow and blue to make green, moisten the 13mm Just Green ribbon with clean water and paint it along its length with a wide, stiff brush (see page 15). Paint the 7mm and 4mm Just Green ribbon in the same way. Leave the ribbons to dry and press them.

Stems and leaves

Note: the leaves are worked in ribbon stitch, reverse ribbon stitch and straight stitch, as indicated on the template.

6 Make up the stem thread using two strands each of Deep Moss, Just Green and Sand embroidery threads and knot one end. Bring the thread up at the base of stem 1 (A) and work a straight stitch, taking a strand of Deep Moss and a strand of Sand through to the back of the fabric at B, one strand of Just Green at C, one strand of Sand at D and the last two strands at E. Couch the stem in position with a toning thread then fasten off all the threads.

7 Using 4mm dyed green ribbon, work the three tiny ribbon stitch leaves at the top of stem 1. Fasten off. Work the 7mm leaves at D in the same way.

8 Work the remaining leaves on stem 1 using 13mm dyed green ribbon, this time anchoring off the ribbon as each leaf is worked.

9 Work stem 2 in the same way (steps 6–8).

Painting the leaves

10 Mix yellow and red fabric paint and a little blue silk paint to make a reddish brown. Do not dilute. Starting with the largest leaf at the base of stem 1, and using a needle to support the ribbon, paint in the centre vein from the base towards the tip, then the finer side veins. Use a fine-pointed brush. Leave to dry.

11 Mix blue and yellow silk paint with a tiny spot of red to make a brown-green. Starting at the top and working one leaf at a time, moisten a leaf with clean water and gently darken the shaded areas to create depth.

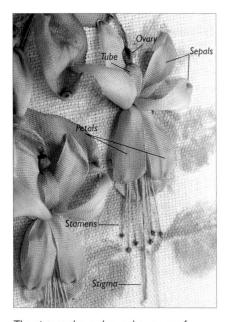

The picture above shows the names of the various flower parts referred to in the instructions.

Completing stem 1

Flowers

Note: for each flower, refer to the basic flower diagram on page 64 and follow the instructions. Where more than one stitch passes through the same point, avoid taking the needle through the same hole each time – place each stitch a thread away from the previous one.

12 Using 7mm Purple ribbon, anchor the ribbon at A (shown on the diagram) and work a straight stitch at B, noting the angle of the second needle. Repeat for C-D and E-F, then bring the needle up again at A. Lay the ribbon over B, place the eye-end of the second needle across it at G, fold the ribbon over the needle and work a straight stitch back at A. Taking care not to twist the ribbon on the wrong side of the fabric, bring it up through at C, fold the ribbon at H and work a reverse left ribbon stitch back at C. Similarly, work a reverse right ribbon stitch at E. Fasten off.

13 For the sepals, use 7mm Soft Poppy ribbon. Anchor the ribbon at C and work a reverse centre ribbon stitch at X, allowing the ribbon to curve as marked on the template. Work a centre ribbon stitch from A at Y, then a centre ribbon stitch from E at Z. Fasten off.

14 The tube is worked first, from top to bottom as a straight stitch using 4mm Soft Poppy ribbon. The ovary is worked in the same way using 4mm Deep Green ribbon.

15 Use two strands of Fuchsia Pink thread to make the stigma, and work a single straight stitch from the top, then a two-loop French knot at the tip.

16 Work the stamens in the same way, using a single strand of Fuchsia Pink, and work a pink two-loop French knot at the base of each one. Ensure you work the stamens from a point at the base of the flower.

17 To shape the flower, thread a single strand of toning Deep Rose thread into a fine needle and knot one end. Bring the needle up just to the right of I, pass the eye-end of the needle through the three loops and take the needle down just to the left of G. Gently pull the thread to place the petals and fasten off.

Buds

18 Using the 7mm Soft Poppy ribbon, work each bud as a single, small straight stitch from the base to pad the petal (see page 28), then a longer reverse centre ribbon stitch over the top to the tip. Fasten off. Work the tube and ovary as before (see step 14).

Flower and bud stems

19 Using a strand each of Just Green and Maroon, wax the thread and work a curved straight stitch from the main stem to each flower and bud (do not couch in place). Fasten off.

Stem 1 flower.

Completing stem 2

Flowers

20 For the petals, work straight stitches in 7mm Pink ribbon. Begin with the two longer base petals, then work the two shorter petals through these so they curve gently over the top to give the flower form. Fasten off.

21 Use 7mm Just Pink ribbon for the sepals, working the two, flatter, inner ones as centre ribbon stitches and the two, looser, outer ones as curved reverse centre ribbon stitches. Fasten off.

Buds

22 Work the buds as before (see step 18) using 7mm Just Pink ribbon. The tiny buds at the top of the stem are worked using 4mm Just Pink ribbon, with the smallest one at the tip pulled a little tighter. Work the tube for these small buds using 2mm Deep Green ribbon.

23 Before working the stigma and stamens, paint the flowers and buds. Dilute a little raspberry silk paint, moisten the tips of the bottom two petals and paint them, taking care not to let the paint seep into the background fabric (see pages 14 and 17). Leave to dry, then paint the tips of the top two petals and the tube. Allow to dry.

24 Paint the base of the sepals in the same way, leave to dry then moisten them again and paint the tips using a dilute pale green mix. Paint the buds pink at the top and pale green at the tips.

25 The stigma and stamens are worked as before (see steps 15 and 16) but with Pink thread. Work a white, two-loop French knot for the stigma and Deep Rose French knots for the stamens.

26 For the flower and bud stems, use a strand each of Deep Moss and Just Green.

27 Using a strand each of Deep Moss and Just Green, work three straight stitches, with the longest in the centre, for a cluster of buds at the top of the painted stem.

Stem 2 flowers.

These fuchsias are different simply because different coloured ribbons have been used; they have all been embroidered following the instructions on pages 64–67.

— reverse ribbon stitch

⟍ angle and position of
second needle

Galanthus

When it is cold and perhaps snowy towards the end of winter, the delicate, little white flowers of the snowdrop appear and hang like lanterns suspended in mid air. They naturalise easily in hedgerows and on the banks of streams, and once established can be found in woodlands spread like a carpet below the trees.

The straight stitch petals are worked on a lightly shaded background with the ribbon pulled over the eye-end of a second needle to shape their tips. The flowers are worked in order, the ones in the background first then those in the foreground worked over the ones beneath.

The template, half actual size; enlarge to 200 per cent. Transfer the design once you have painted the background. Mark both ends of the petals (A-B, D-E and F-G on the diagram), the calyx and the base of each stem, then lightly draw in the connecting lines for the two outer petals only.

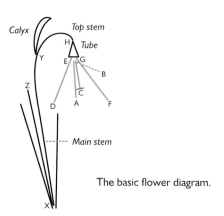

2.66m (105in) 7mm White (No. 03)

0.33m (13in) 4mm Soft Green (No. 33)

3m (118½in) 4mm Just Green (No. 31)

The basic flower diagram.

Calyx *Top stem* H *Tube* Y E G B Z C D A F *Main stem* X

37 x 32cm (14½ x 12½in) linen/cotton fabric; 2m (79in) white stranded thread to match the background fabric; 1m (39½in) white coton à broder; silk paints in navy blue and primary yellow; fabric paints in cobalt blue, buttercup yellow and cardinal red.

Painting the fabric

1 Mix blue and yellow silk paint on a tile to make a very pale green, then moisten the fabric and lightly shade the lower third (see page 18). While the paint is still wet, drag a few strokes up to within 1cm (½in) of the top. Leave to dry.

Note: remove any excess colour by pressing it with a piece of absorbent kitchen paper or iron it between two pieces of absorbent scrap fabric (see page 15).

Painting the ribbon and threads

2 Cut a 50cm (19¾in) length of white stranded thread and put it to one side. Make the remaining stranded thread and the coton à broder into loose skeins.

3 Mix blue and yellow silk paint to make a blue-green shade and dilute it slightly. Moisten both skeins of thread with clean water then dye them to a mid blue-green. Leave to dry.

4 Cut a 50cm (19¾in) length of 4mm Just Green ribbon and put it to one side. Moisten the rest of the Just Green ribbon and randomly dye it with the remaining blue-green paint to create a shaded effect (see page 15). Allow to dry and press.

5 Mix blue silk paint with yellow and a tiny spot of red fabric paint to make a slightly more yellowy brown-green shade. Take the 50cm (19¾in) length of 4mm Just Green ribbon and, keeping it taut, use a dry, fine brush to paint some short, fine lines along its length. Dry and press.

Flowers

Note: to suggest movement, each flower is a little different. For each flower, refer to the basic flower diagram on the left and follow the instructions below, using the picture of the embroidery to determine the number and order of the petals. Work the flowers in the order indicated by the numbers on the template.

6 Anchor a length of 7mm White ribbon at A on flower 1. Work a straight stitch at B, pulling the ribbon over the eye-end of a second needle to create a rounded petal tip. Using the template as a guide, bring the needle up through the ribbon at C and work a straight stitch to just above B, lifting the ribbon to sit over the first petal. Work petals D-E and F-G as A-B to sit over the petals just worked. Fasten off.

7 Using the 4mm Soft Green ribbon, work a tiny straight stitch from H to B, pulling the ribbon over a second needle at B. Fasten off.

8 Complete flowers 2 and 3 in the same way.

Stems and calyxes

9 Make up a stem thread using four strands of dyed green thread. Thread it into a medium-sized needle, knot one end and wax the thread from the knot end.

10 Bring the thread up at the base of the stem of flower 1 (X) and take it back down at the base of the calyx (Y). Couch the thread down to curve the stem (see page 40) and fasten off. Repeat for flowers 2 and 3.

11 Use the 4mm dyed striped ribbon for the calyx. Knot one end, moisten your thumb and forefinger and crease the ribbon lengthways for approximately 0.75cm (¼in) from the knot. Bring the ribbon through at Y and work a curved centre ribbon stitch that will fit round the top stem. Fasten off.

12 Work the top stem as a straight stitch from Y to H using the green dyed coton à broder. Couch it down to form a curve (see page 40). Fasten off.

Leaves

13 Cut a length of 4mm randomly dyed green ribbon. Thread it into a needle and bring it up at X. Work a centre ribbon stitch to Z and fasten off. Work the other two leaves, referring to the picture to bend and twist them into the right position.

Completing the flowers

14 Complete flowers 4 to 7 first (including their stems and leaves), then the remainder of the flowers (8 to 11).

Painting the petals and leaves

15 Mix a little blue and yellow fabric paint to make a deep green. Do not add water. Use a dry, fine brush to paint an inverted V shape on the short petal in the middle of each flower. Hold the petals to one side if necessary using the eye-end of a needle. Leave to dry.

Note: to prevent paint seeping into the background fabric, only moisten the ribbon and shade it up to a point 0.5cm (¼in) from where it passes through the fabric. The same applies to ribbon that is worked through another stitch.

16 Mix a mid to deep blue-green using silk paint. Do not add water. Starting with the background leaves, use a fine brush to lightly moisten each leaf in turn and then paint along one edge to give a shaded effect.

17 Add a hint of red paint to the blue-green mix and dilute it to make a very pale grey tone. Test the colour on a spare piece of ribbon before applying it to your embroidery. Moisten a petal then subtly shade the lower edge just above the tip. Paint the remaining petals in the same way.

Hydrangea

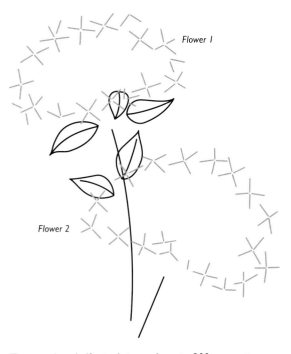

Flower 1

Flower 2

The template, half actual size; enlarge to 200 per cent. Transfer the design before painting the background. Mark the positions of the leaves, the base of each stem and the petals of each flower. Lightly draw in the leaves and connecting lines for the petals.

10m (395in) 7mm Just Pink (No. 05)

0.33m (13in) 13mm Just Green (No. 31)

33 x 35cm (13 x 13¾in) linen/cotton fabric; stranded threads in Deep Moss (No. 268), Moss (No. 266), Just Green (No. 859), Delph Blue (No. 118) and a white thread to match the background fabric; silk paints in magenta, navy blue and primary yellow; white fabric paint.

Small, four-petalled flowers are clustered together to create these beautiful, very large and showy flowers. This variety is known as a mop head; the lace cap, another variety, is equally as large but with a mass of tiny flowers in the centre surrounded by a circle of the same, four-petalled flowers. They make an impact not only in the garden, but cut as fresh flowers or dried, sometimes painted, in large flower arrangements.

One shade of 7mm Just Pink ribbon has been dyed two shades, a lilac pink and a little deeper lilac blue to create light and shade. You could alter these tones to your favourite shades.

Painting the background

1 Mix together a little yellow and blue silk paint on a tile to make a mid green, and magenta and blue to a make pink-mauve. Dilute both mixes with a little water. Place the background fabric in an embroidery frame and moisten the area within one of the flowerheads as far as the centres of the outer flowers, allowing the water to spread outwards from there. Paint on a little of each colour at random. Repeat for the other flowerhead and allow to dry.

Painting the ribbon

2 Cut a 6m (237in) length of 7mm Just Pink ribbon. Mix magenta silk paint with a hint of blue and dilute with water to make a lilac pink. Moisten the ribbon and dye it patchily (see page 15). Dry and press.

3 Mix the same colours to make a deeper lilac blue and dye the remaining 4m (158in) length of 7mm Just Pink ribbon in the same way.

Flower 1

Stem

4 Use three strands each of Moss and Deep Moss, and one strand of Just Green. Thread them into a medium-sized needle, knot one end and work the main stem from the flower to the base. Fasten off behind the stem. Couch the threads down to curve the stem.

Leaves

5 Using 13mm Just Green ribbon, work each of the leaves either side of the flowerhead as a centre ribbon stitch and the half leaf in the centre as a straight stitch. Complete the leaves by working the two lower ones as centre ribbon stitches.

Painting the leaves

6 Mix blue and yellow silk paints to make a light and a dark green. Add a little light green to a spot of white fabric paint and, using a fine paintbrush, draw in the vein lines. Leave to dry. Moisten a leaf with clean water and paint it using the lighter shade for the veins and the darker green for the leaf itself. Paint the remaining leaves in the same way. Leave to dry.

Flowerhead

Note: use the dyed Just Pink ribbon for all of the flowers; refer to the picture for placing the different colours and shapes of flower. Some of the flowers, in particular around the outside, are oval in shape, having only two, three or occasionally single petals. These create the overall shape of the flowerhead.

Work the petals around the outside of the flowerhead first. Avoid taking the ribbon across the back of the flower.

7 Each flower is made up of four straight stitches. Bring the needle up at the tip of the first petal and down at the centre of the flower, using the eye-end of a second needle to control the ribbon and shape the petal. Work the remaining three petals in the same way, taking care not to stitch into the ribbon on the wrong side. Fasten off.

Note: fasten off each flower before starting the next, otherwise the ribbon will twist and the petal shapes become distorted.

8 When you have worked the flowers around the outside, spiral in towards the centre. Position the flowers at slightly different angles to avoid gaps, and as you approach the centre place some petals so they partly overlap another to give the flowerhead a slightly domed appearance. Partly overlap the top of the stem and the leaves as well.

9 Make a stem thread using two strands of Deep Moss, one of Moss and one of Just Green thread. Work the four small stems at the top of the main stem as straight stitches, tucking them under and between the leaves and petals. Fasten off.

10 Using one strand of each colour, work some tiny straight stitch stems at random between the flowers.

11 For the flower centres, thread a single strand of Delph Blue thread into a fine needle and knot one end. Bring the needle up through a petal, 2mm (⅛in) from the centre, and back down at the centre. Pass a stitch through the other three petals in the same way, making sure they meet at the centre point to form a cross. Work the remaining flowers to complete the flowerhead.

Flower 2

12 Work as for flower 1, but add the main stem over the top of the flowers at the base when the flowerhead is complete.

To finish

13 Use the eye-end of a size 18 needle to lift all the petals (see page 41).

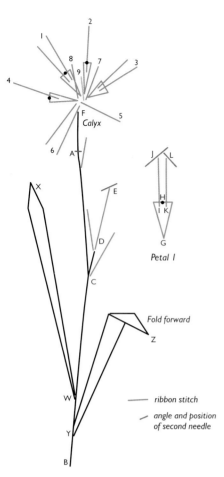

The template, half actual size; enlarge to 200 per cent. Mark the six petals (1–6), points A, B and C on the main stem and the two ends of the bud (D-E).

—— ribbon stitch

⁄ angle and position of second needle

1m (39½in) 13mm White (No. 03)

0.33m (13in) 7mm White (No. 03)

0.33m (13in) 4mm White (No. 03)

0.5m (19¾in) 13mm Just Green (No. 31)

0.5m (19¾in) 7mm Just Green (No. 31)

38 x 43cm (15 x 17in) linen/cotton fabric; stranded threads in Just Green (No. 859), Soft Apple Green (No. 264) and a white thread to match the background fabric; silk paints in navy blue, poppy red and buttercup yellow; fabric paints in white and buttercup yellow.

Iris

These colourful, quite spectacular flowers with their strong, straight stems range in height from 5 to 150cm (2 to 60in) or more. They have sword-like leaves that remain well after the flowering period and a variety can be found for most gardens. The flowers can be a single colour or a variety of colours, ranging from white to almost black; from creams and yellows to rich, coppery brown; blues, pinks and mauves to deep purple.

The basic flower is formed from a triangle of three large outer petals (falls) with three slightly smaller petals (standards) between them, and embroidered with 13mm ribbon.

Petal 1

1 Using 7mm White ribbon, fold one end in half lengthwise, thread it into a needle and anchor it at the base of the petal, G (see page 22). Using the eye-end of a second needle to control the ribbon, work a straight stitch at H to form the shank.

2 Take the end of a length of 13mm White ribbon down through the shank at I, anchor it and work a straight stitch at J (note the angle of the second needle). Fasten off. Now anchor the ribbon at K and work a straight stitch at L. Make sure that the edges of both stitches sit side-by-side to make a single petal.

Petal 2

3 Using 4mm White ribbon work the shank as a straight stitch, as in step 1. Fasten off. Using 13mm White ribbon work the petal as a reverse right ribbon stitch, using a cotton bud to pull the ribbon over and shape the petal tip.

Petals 3 to 6

4 Work petal 3 as petal 1; petal 4 as petal 2; petal 5 as petal 2, but without the shank; and petal 6 as petal 1, again without the shank.

Painting petals 1–6

Note: take care to retain the petals' shapes during and after painting.

To hold the petals to one side and keep both hands free for painting, place the embroidered flower area on a foam pad and position glass-headed pins, pushed through the fabric and into the foam, to hold the petals not being painted away from those that are (see page 17). When the petals you are painting are dry, reposition the pins and repeat.

5 Beginning with petal 2, use white fabric paint to paint a centre line from the base of the shank to approximately 1cm (½in) from the tip of the petal. Leave to dry. Moisten the ribbon with clean water then paint the petal using blue silk paint. With a clean, moist brush touch the petal lightly where it is fullest to remove some of the colour from the petal and create a highlight. Leave to dry. Using buttercup yellow fabric paint, paint a fine line along the centre of the white line. Paint petals 4 and 5 in the same way.

6 Paint in the centre white line of petal 1 (see step 5) and leave to dry. Moisten the petal and use blue silk paint to paint the shank and outer one-third of the petal, leaving the centre area free of paint. Remove a little of the colour using a moist, clean brush (see step 5). Referring to the picture, use buttercup yellow fabric paint to paint the yellow area through the centre of the petal. When dry, mix a spot each of white fabric paint and blue silk paint to lightly paint in the fine vein lines. Leave to dry. Paint petals 3 and 6 in the same way.

Petals 7 to 9

7 Work petal 7 from the base, using 7mm White ribbon, as a left ribbon stitch. Curve the stitch inwards towards the centre of the flower to sit it on its side. Fasten off. Work petal 8 as a right ribbon stitch and curve it inwards towards petal 7. Fasten off. Petal 9 is a reverse centre ribbon stitch, made a little shorter and rounder than petals 7 and 8. Fasten off.

Painting petals 7–9

8 Paint petals 7–9 with blue silk paint, then lighten the top of the curve on each petal with a moist brush.

Painting the ribbon for the leaves

9 Mix blue and buttercup yellow silk paint to make a mid to deep green. Moisten the 7mm Just Green ribbon and paint it (see page 16). Repeat for the 13mm Just Green ribbon, then draw a clean, moist brush along the centre to lighten it slightly. Dry and press both ribbons.

Stem

10 Make up a stem thread with four Soft Apple Green and eight Just Green threads, and knot them together at one end. Wax the thread from the knot upwards to flatten it and thread it into a size 18 needle. Bring the needle up at A and down at B, placing the eye-end of a second needle underneath to pull the thread over and lay it flat. Bring the needle up at C and down at D. Fasten off. Use a strand of toning thread to secure the main stem at C.

Calyx

11 Using 7mm dyed green ribbon, work a straight stitch from A to F. Fasten off.

Bud

12 Anchor the end of a 12cm (4¾in) length of 13mm White ribbon at D, then anchor another length through the same hole to sit on top. Place the first ribbon so the right selvedge just covers E and put a pin in at this point. Thread the second ribbon into a large needle and work a reverse centre ribbon stitch through the first ribbon at E, removing the pin first, then gently pull the ribbon

to create a bud shape. Fasten off. Thread the first ribbon into a large needle and work a right ribbon stitch at E, noting the angle of the second needle, so that it rolls from behind and just over the centre edge of the first stitch to form the bud. Fasten off.

13 Paint the bud using blue silk paint, leaving the centre area of the right-hand petal white. Shade the centre of the white area with a touch of pale yellow silk paint, then with a clean brush moisten the curved blue area to remove some of the colour.

Leaves

14 Using 7mm dyed green ribbon, take the ribbon through at the base of the top leaf (just below the calyx) and angle it so that it sits over the stem. Work a centre ribbon stitch at the tip so that the ribbon wraps round the stem. Repeat for the two leaves below the bud.

15 Fold one end of the 13mm dyed green ribbon in half lengthwise and thread it into a needle, as in step 1. Anchor it at W and work a reverse centre ribbon stitch at X. Fasten off. Using a toning green thread and a fine needle, work a tiny stitch to pull the left edge of the ribbon in place over the base of the stem.

16 For the right-hand leaf, anchor the ribbon at Y, bend the ribbon forwards (as shown on the template) and work a centre ribbon stitch at Z. Fasten off. Refold the ribbon and secure the right-hand edge as in step 15.

Painting

Note: when painting long, flat pieces of ribbon, slide a piece of thin, white card between the ribbon and the fabric to prevent paint getting on to the fabric.

17 Make a deep green with blue and yellow silk paint, moisten the long, left-hand leaf and paint a line down both selvedges. Paint the right-hand leaf along the back edge only in the same way.

18 Paint the edges of the small leaves as in step 17, then mix a spot of red into the green to make a browny green. Moisten and shade the lower part of each one. Leave to dry.

Jasminum

On a grey day in winter, the bright yellow, star-like flowers of the winter-flowering jasmine growing on the north wall of my home are a joy. Not really a climber or a shrub but somewhere in-between, myriads of small flowers are borne on long, straight, green, twiggy stems.

Five evenly spaced petals are worked in straight stitch with 4mm yellow ribbon after the stem has been embroidered. The buds and calyx are then lightly shaded and a spot of colour is placed in the centre of each flower.

Stems

Note: to anchor the thread at the base of a stem, make a knot 10cm (4in) from the end. This allows the stem to be re-tensioned if necessary and the tail sewn behind the stem line when the embroidery is finished. Cut off the excess.

1 Using six strands of Deep Moss embroidery thread (do not separate the strands), bring the thread up at the base of stem 1 (A) and lay it in position along the length of the stem. Take two of the strands through to the back at B and couch A-B in position with a strand of toning thread. Take two more strands through at C, one strand through at D and the final strand through to the back at E. Tension the stem, couch it in position and fasten off each thread.

2 The side stems are worked using four strands of Deep Moss thread. Start at the main stem and reduce to two then one strand at the points marked on the template (see step 1).

3 Replace template accurately, transfer stem 2 and repeat steps 1 and 2.

Stem 1

Stem 2

calyx/tube

The template, half actual size; enlarge to 200 per cent. Begin by marking stem 1 by a series of fine dots. Remove the template and embroider this stem. Repeat for stem 2. Replace the template again and mark the centre and tips of alternate flowers and buds along each stem. Lightly draw in these petals. If you wish, the remaining flowers and buds can then be transferred as before, or you may prefer to work these by eye.

5m (197½in) 4mm Yellow (No. 15)

2m (79in) 2mm Yellow (No. 15)

2m (79in) 2mm Khaki (No. 56)

40 x 30cm (15¾ x 11¾in) linen/cotton fabric; stranded threads in Deep Moss (No. 268) and a white thread to match the background fabric; silk paints in navy blue, poppy red and primary yellow.

Flowers

Note: work the petals of those flowers you have marked first, then work the others either by eye or by replacing the template and transferring the remaining petals.

4 For the open flowers, thread a length of 4mm Yellow ribbon into a size 18 needle and knot one end. Bring the needle up at the tip of one petal and, using the eye-end of a second needle to control and lift the ribbon, work a straight stitch down at the centre of the flower. Bring the needle up at the tip of the next petal and repeat for the remaining five petals. Fasten off.

Note: do not take all the petals down through the same hole in the centre of the flower as they will overlap, and avoid stitching through any ribbon at the centre.

5 Stitch the calyxes (that join the flowers to the stems) using the 2mm Khaki ribbon and a size 24 needle. Work each one as a short straight stitch from the stem. Fasten off, then with the 2mm Yellow ribbon work another short straight stitch from the calyx to the base of the flower for the tube.

Note: some of the calyxes have only a tube at the end, and no flower; others have a straight stitch bud.

6 Using a single strand of green thread, work the pairs of tiny straight stitches at the top of some stems (see template). Using 2mm Khaki ribbon, work the trio of tiny ribbon stitches at the top of stem 1 and the lower left stem.

Painting the flowers

7 Mix a little yellow, blue and red silk paint to make a browny red (do not dilute it). Use a dry, fine paintbrush with just a little paint on the tip to touch the tips and centres of the petals.

8 Make the paint slightly redder and first paint one edge of the calyx, then place a fine line down one side of the tube as a shadow to complete the embroidery.

Kniphofia

It is plain to see why this is commonly called a red hot poker, with its fiery orange and red tubular flowers creating a dense spike at the top of a strong stem. Forming large clumps of coarse, grass-like leaves, it is both loved and loathed by gardeners. Some varieties can reach up to 1.8m (72in) high, and there are now newer, cultivated varieties as small as 50cm (20in) high in numerous tones from white and green to yellow and red.

To create the shape, the straight stitch petals are worked over a padded base with 4mm yellow ribbon. These are then shaded before working the remainder of the flower with 4mm soft orange ribbon.

Painting the silk habitai

1 Mix blue, yellow and a spot of red silk paint to make a browny green and paint the shape of the padded area. Allow the paint to spread beyond the dotted outline. Leave to dry and press.

Attaching the silk habitai to the background fabric

2 Allowing an extra 2cm (¾in) around the edge, cut out the shape of the padded area from the silk habitai. Also cut a piece of wadding the same size as the padded area.

3 Place the wadding on the fabric, with the silk in place on top, and hold them in position with two or three loose tacking stitches.

4 Carefully fold the edges of the silk under the wadding and secure them with pins. Avoid compressing the wadding too tightly. Slip stitch the silk in position using a toning thread.

Note: it is easier to prepare and stitch 2 to 3cm (about 1in) at a time.

Flowerhead

5 Thread a length of 4mm Yellow ribbon into a large needle and knot one end. Referring to the template, work petal 1 as a straight stitch from the base of the petal to the tip. Bring the needle up at the base of petal 2 and repeat. Work all the petals in order round to petal 9.

The template, half actual size; enlarge to 200 per cent. Transfer the outline of the padded area, the outer petals (1–10), the stem and the leaves. Also transfer the shape of the padded area (as a dotted outline) on to the silk habitai.

4m of 4mm Yellow (No. 15)

6m of 4mm Soft Orange (No. 16)

1m of 7mm Just Green (No. 31)

28 x 38cm (11 x 15in) linen/cotton fabric; 10 x 14cm (4 x 5½in) silk habitai; 10 x 3cm (4 x 1¼in) wadding; stranded threads in Deep Moss (No. 268), Just Green (No. 859), Soft Brown (No. 904) and a white thread to match the background fabric; silk paints in navy blue, poppy red and primary yellow.

6 Now work petals 10 to 17 in the same way, so that they sit slightly above the previous row of petals.

7 Support petal 1 with the eye-end of a needle, and use a fine paintbrush to moisten it with clean water. Paint from the base downwards with undiluted red silk paint, stopping 5mm (¼in) from the tip. Paint petals 2 to 9 in the same way. Allow them to dry then paint petals 10 to 17.

Note: a hairdryer is useful to speed up drying time and to stop paint travelling too far and/or seeping into the background fabric.

8 Referring to the picture, use the 4mm Yellow ribbon to work a few petals in the middle of the flower just above the second row, then work a third row of petals slightly overlapping the second. Paint these petals as before and leave them to dry.

9 Using 4mm Soft Orange ribbon, work two more rows and then paint the petals as before.

10 Cut the rest of the 4mm Soft Orange ribbon into manageable lengths (for example, 1 to 1.5m, or 40 to 60in), then paint each length with red silk paint. Allow some shading to occur, rather than trying to achieve an even colour. Dry the ribbon and press.

11 Use the red dyed ribbon to work the remaining petals. Gradually make the outer base petals smaller and tighter as you move up the flowerhead; use progressively smaller loops for the centre petals.

Note how the angles of the petals vary as you move up the flower – the outer ones radiate outwards at an increasingly wider angle, becoming almost horizontal at the top. Take care and time to place all the stitches carefully.

Stem

12 Make up the stem thread with eight Deep Moss, four Just Green and two Soft Brown strands. Knot one end. Thoroughly moisten a piece of soap and pull the thread over the soap from the knot end. Thread it into a large needle. Bring the thread up between the petals at the top of the stem, flatten the length between your index finger and thumb, then take the needle down at the base of the stem, pulling the threads over the eye-end of a second needle to flatten the end.

Leaves

13 Use a medium hot iron to press a crease along the length of the 7mm Just Green ribbon. Mix yellow and blue silk paint to make green, open up the ribbon and then moisten and paint it. Leave to dry. Mix a darker green, then moisten the ribbon with a clean, damp brush and paint along one selvedge. Leave to dry then press the ribbon open.

14 Using the dyed green ribbon work a centre ribbon stitch from A to B and fasten off. Work a centre ribbon stitch for C-D, folding the ribbon over the eye-end of a second needle to place the fold and tension the ribbon before completing the stitch at D. Fasten off, then use a toning thread to work a tiny stitch through the selvedge at the back of the fold to keep the ribbon taut and make it sit at a right angle to the fabric. Fasten off. Work leaf E-F in the same way to complete the embroidery.

The different varieties of Kniphofia shown on the left are slightly smaller with less densely packed petals.

Lathyrus

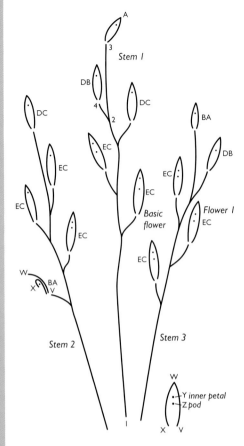

The template, half actual size; enlarge to 200 per cent. Mark with a dot the top and bottom of each flower, and the point where each side stem joins one of the three main stems. Remove the template and lightly draw in the shapes for the flowers as they appear on the template.

Note: the first letter of the two-letter codes marked on the template indicates which length of ribbon to use for the outer petals; the second letter indicates which length to use for the inner petals

2.5m (98¾in) 13mm White (No. 03)

0.75m (29½in) 7mm White (No. 03)

1m (39½in) 2mm Moss (No. 20)

40 x 33cm (15¾ x 13in) linen/cotton fabric; stranded threads in Green (No. 216), Just Green (No. 859), White (No. 2), Pale Pink (No. 73) and a white thread to match the background fabric; silk paints in navy blue, magenta and primary yellow.

Masses of large, delicate flowers, mostly perfumed, on long, slender stems, in the widest range of colours imaginable. What more could anyone ask for? They look beautiful in the garden and are often grown for cut flowers – the more they are cut the more flowers they produce.

Also known as sweet pea, the pea-like flowers are all worked with 13mm white ribbon. The larger back petal is worked first, then the slightly smaller inner petal, with a small pod-shaped petal in the centre of the larger flowers. When finished, each spray is shaded a different colour.

Stitching the ribbon

Note: only cut the 13mm ribbon after each piece is stitched; it is much easier to hold a long length while stitching.

Using a coloured thread to gather the ribbon and a fabric-coloured thread to secure it to the fabric prevents the wrong thread being cut in error.

1 Thread a fine needle with a length of Pale Pink thread and knot one end. Cut the end of the 13mm White ribbon at an angle. Referring to page 32, anchor the thread over the selvedge of the ribbon 1.5cm (¾in) from the end. Work a line of tiny running stitches across at an angle, then for 10cm (4in) along the selvedge, then back across at an angle again.

2 Do not fasten off or cut the thread, but cut the ribbon 1.5cm (¾in) from the stitching line and use a fine pencil to mark the code given below (E) on the tag end. Stitch another length with an 8cm (3in) line of running stitches, mark code C on the end then pin a tag end of each ribbon together to make a pair.

3 Stitch more lengths of White ribbon in the same way, with varying lengths of stitching, as indicated below. Mark each length with the relevant code.

3 x 5.5cm (2in) lengths (A)
4 x 6cm (2¼in) lengths (B)
10 x 8cm (3in) lengths (C)
4 x 9cm (3½in) lengths (D)
8 x 10cm (4in) lengths (E)

Fold each length of ribbon exactly in half widthways and press to crease (the way you do this depends on whether you are right- or left-handed – see the diagrams below).

Right-handed   Left-handed

Flower 1

Note: never stitch through any gathering stitches. When the petal is stitched in position the gathering thread is gently pulled again to 'seat' the gathers before fastening off the thread.

4 Begin by working the outer petal. Referring to the instructions on page 32, take ribbon E

that you stitched in step 1 and, using a white thread, anchor the knot end of the ribbon at V (see diagram next to template). Bring the anchoring thread up at W and work a tiny stitch over the gathering line at the fold. Keep the thread to one side. Take the other tag end through at X, leave the gathering thread at the front and secure the ribbon as before. Bring the anchoring thread to the front at V. Gently pull the gathering thread to fit the petal line, placing slightly more gathers at the base of the petal.

5 Use the anchoring thread to stab stitch the ribbon in place on the petal line. Fasten off. Pull the gathering thread gently to 'seat' the gathers and fasten off the gathering thread securely.

6 Anchor the inner petal, ribbon C, in the same place as ribbon E, but with the fold line at Y, and pull the gathering thread as before (step 4). Now lay the petal across the centre to the left and stab stitch along the outer edge V-Y, then lay it the other way to stitch Y-X. Seat the gathers and secure as before (step 5).

Note: stitching the outer edge of the inner petal will keep the petal upright and partly conceal the centre.

7 For the centre pod use 7mm White ribbon and secure one end at V. Fold it at Z and take it through to the back at X. Tension the ribbon round the eye-end of a needle at Z and secure the lower edge with a tiny stitch. Tension the ribbon to keep the pod upright and fasten off.

Remaining flowers

Note: the flowers all vary in size, and not all have a pod in the centre.

8 Work the remaining flowers in the same way as flower 1, varying the lengths of ribbon used for the inner and outer petals, and angling them as shown in the picture. Follow steps 9 and 10 below for the flower at the top of stem 1 and that at the bottom of stem 2.

9 For the flower at the top of stem 1, secure a length of ribbon A at V, W and X, and attach the right-hand side of the petal as in steps 4 and 5. Now lay the flower to the right and secure the outer edge.

10 For the flower at the bottom of stem 2, anchor a length of ribbon B at V and W, pull the gathering thread and stab stitch the ribbon in position so that the top of the petal, with less gathers, curves back on itself, as shown on the template. Use a length of ribbon A to work the smaller inner petal, curving it downwards. Work the pod as before (step 7).

Stems

11 Put together three strands each of Green and Just Green thread, knot one end and thread it into a needle. Bring the thread up at the base of stem 1 and lay it in position. Take three strands only down at 2 and fasten off. Use the remaining three strands to work the top of the stem (2–3) and fasten off. Use a toning thread to couch down and shape the stem. Work the side stems in the same way, using only three strands of either green thread, to complete stem 1.

12 Work stems 2 and 3 in the same way.

Calyxes

13 Using 2mm Moss ribbon, work a tiny straight stitch either side of the stem at the base of each flower.

Painting the petals

14 Using silk paint, mix the magenta with a touch of yellow for the flowers on stem 1, and dilute with water to create the required shade. Refer to the section on painting petals on page 17.

15 Start with the lowest flower on stem 1. Using clean water and a fine brush, moisten the edge of the outer petal. Hold the ribbon away from the fabric and the other flowers with the eye-end of a needle, pick up a little of the colour and brush the paint on to the edge of the petal only. The colour will spread and gradually fade away towards the centre of the flower. For more colour, paint around the edge again. Allow the petal to dry, then repeat for the inner petal, avoiding the inner pod.

16 Paint the remaining flowers on stem 1. Dilute the paint a little more and apply to the inner pods.

17 Paint the flowers on stems 2 and 3 in the same way, using blue with a little magenta for stem 2 and very pale magenta only for stem 3.

Lavandula

Lavender, with its uniquely scented flowers, has been much loved for generations and is just as popular today. Lavender oil, the basis of many perfumes, also has numerous medical qualities. Flowers are cut, dried and hung in bunches to perfume a room or put into little decorative bags and placed in drawers and cupboards to scent linen and underwear. The cluster of tightly packed flowers, from white to pink and lavender to purple, sit at the tops of the stems, and the silver grey leaves are also scented.

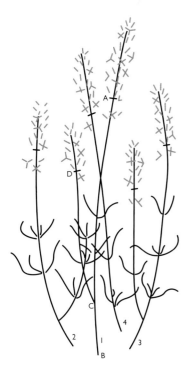

The template, half actual size; enlarge to 200 per cent. Mark a few dots along the stem lines as a guide only. Remove the template and work the stems (steps 1 and 2). Replace the template accurately, and transfer both flowerheads of stem 1. Partly remove the template and lightly draw in the petal lines. Replace the template and repeat for the remaining flowerheads. (You may prefer to transfer just a few flowers on each stem, and to refer to the picture and template to add the remainder by eye when you start to stitch.)

1.5m (59¼in) 4mm Light Mauve (No. 178)

1.5m (59¼in) 4mm Mid Mauve (No. 179)

1.5m (59¼in) 4mm Just Lilac (No. 83)

2m (79in) 2mm Cream (No. 156)

28 x 33cm (11 x 13in) linen/cotton fabric; stranded threads in Just Green (No. 859) and a white thread to match the background fabric; silk paints in navy blue, magenta, poppy red and primary yellow.

Stems

1 Using six strands of Just Green for the stem thread, thread it into a needle and knot one end. Bring the needle up at A at the top of stem 1, down at B, up again at C and down at D. Couch the stems in place, connecting the main stem at C, with a single strand of the same colour thread. Fasten off all the threads.

2 Work stems 2 and 3 in the same way as stem 1, and work stem 4 from the base to the top.

3 Using two strands of Just Green thread, work a straight stitch at the top of stems 1–3 to complete.

Painting the ribbons

4 Mix magenta and blue silk paint to make a deep mauve and dilute it slightly. Crumple the three 4mm mauve and lilac ribbons in your fingers and dab them with the paint leaving some areas bare. Add drips of clean water to the paint-free areas. Leave to dry.

5 Mix yellow and blue silk paints to make two greens then add a touch of red to one of them. Dilute both mixes a little and use them to dye the 2mm Cream ribbon as in step 4. Dry and press all the ribbons.

Flowers and buds

Note: the three coloured ribbons are used to create light and shade, with the darkest tone suggesting shadow and the palest tone suggesting light. Refer to the picture to place the colours.

6 Thread a length of ribbon into a needle and knot one end. Start at the base of a flower and work each petal as a straight stitch from the tip to the centre of the flower. The buds are single straight stitches worked from the tip to the base. Embroider the lower flowers and buds first, then anchor off before working the next section up. Complete all the flowers and buds.

Leaves

7 Using 2mm dyed green ribbon, thread a length into a size 24 needle and knot one end. Starting with the pair of long leaves at the top of stem 1, bring the needle up at the base of one leaf, allow the ribbon to twist once and take the needle down at the tip. Do not pull the ribbon tight; allow the leaf to twist and bend. Repeat for the second long leaf and fasten off.

8 Work the next pair of long leaves down on the same stem and fasten off.

9 Work the remaining leaves in the same way, starting with those at the back of the embroidery and moving towards the front. Where present, stitch the smaller inner leaves first. Take some leaves behind the stems where necessary.

This blue lavender is a more compact variety, and worked with slightly smaller stitches.

Commonly called French lavender, this variety is easily identified with its tuft of bracts.

The template, half actual size; enlarge to 200 per cent. Transfer the positions of the stems, leaves, petals and bracts. Remove the template and lightly draw in the fan shape only, not the leaf or petal lines.

— leaves

1.5m (59¼in) 7mm Dusky Red (No. 114)

2m (79in) 7mm Moss (No. 20)

0.67m (26½in) 4mm Moss (No. 20)

5m (197½in) 4mm Bright Pink (No. 25)

1.5m (59¼in) 2mm Dark Red (No. 50)

30 x 33cm (11¾ x 13in) linen/cotton fabric; stranded threads in Deep Moss (No. 268), Moss (No. 266), Just Green (No. 859), Deep Red (No. 13), Maroon (No. 44) and a white thread to match the background fabric; silk paints in navy blue, poppy red and primary yellow; fabric paint in white.

Monarda

This attractive, highly aromatic plant, rich in nectar, is a major attraction to bees from midsummer to autumn, and the bright, showy flowers make it a popular border plant. Also known as bergamot, it has strong, tall stems, and each flower is a mass of small tubular petals, looking much like a thistle, which sit above bracts that are usually tinged red. It is, in fact, a very useful herb with leaves that can also be dried and used to make herbal tea.

The petals are twisted straight stitches worked with 4mm ribbon that are allowed to curve, with slightly looser ones placed at the front to create roundness and form. A deeper shade of 7mm ribbon is used for the bracts below.

Flower 1

Flowerhead

Note: steps 1 to 3 are illustrated in the pictures at the bottom of the facing page.

1 Put together a strand each of Just Green, Deep Red and Maroon thread, knot one end and thread it into a needle. Work a fan of long and short straight stitches at the base of flower 1.

2 Thread a length of 2mm Dark Red ribbon into a size 24 needle, knot one end then work long and short straight stitches, some twisted, over and between the thread stitches worked in step 1, leaving the top edge uneven. Fasten off.

3 Using two strands of Maroon and one of Deep Red thread, work two-loop French knots (see page 36) to fill the V shape at the base of the fan.

Note: each petal is a straight stitch with the ribbon twisted two or three times either to the left or to the right to create a fairly loose, slightly raised petal. Curl each one at a different angle and work the longest petals at the back first, using the eye-end of a second needle to place each stitch.

4 Thread a length of 4mm Bright Pink ribbon into a needle and knot one end. Bring the needle up at the base of the centre petal at the back of the flower, twist it two or three times and take the

Petals

Bracts

Leaves

Step 1

Step 2

Step 3

needle down at the tip (see page 28). Referring to the picture, work the petals either side to complete the back row.

5 Work the next row marked on the template, then those further forward, and finally the petals at the front of the flower that bend at different angles. Fasten off.

6 Using 7mm Moss ribbon, work the two centre ribbon stitch leaves from the base of the flowerhead to the tip. Fasten off.

7 For the bracts, use 7mm Dusky Red ribbon; they are a mixture of left, right and centre ribbon stitches tucked in above the leaves at the base of the flower with the tips tilting in different directions. Refer to the picture on the previous page.

Stem

Note: when working a stem from the base, knot the thread 3–4cm (approx. 1½in) from the end to leave a tail. When the embroidery is complete, re-tension the stem, then use a toning thread to secure 1cm (½in) of the tail behind the stem, at the back of the work, to prevent the knot and ends showing through at the front.

8 Make up the stem thread with two Moss and six Deep Moss strands, thread it into a needle and make a knot 3–4cm (approx. 1½in) from one end. Soap the thread from the knot end for the approximate length of the stem. Bring the thread up at the base of the stem and work a straight stitch to the top. Tension the stem and fasten off.

Leaves

9 With 7mm Moss ribbon, work the two pairs of larger ribbon stitch leaves. Fasten off as each leaf is worked. Use the 4mm Moss ribbon to work the two pairs of smaller leaves. Fasten off. Work a tiny stitch with green thread over the stem between each pair of large leaves to position the stem.

Painting the leaves

10 Using white fabric paint and a fine brush, paint a fine central vein and a suggestion of side veins on each of the large green leaves. Leave to dry, then paint over these lines with red silk paint. Leave to dry.

11 Put a little red silk paint on a tile and add a spot of water to dilute it slightly. Moisten one of the two leaves attached to the flowerhead with clean water and apply a little paint at the base of the leaf. Allow the paint to blend towards the tip so that approximately two-thirds of the leaf are shaded red, leaving a green tip. Paint the other leaf in the same way and and leave to dry.

Painting the flowerhead

12 Using white fabric paint and a fine brush, paint a fine central vein about two-thirds of the way along the centre of each bract from the base.

13 Mix a little blue and yellow silk paint to make green then add a spot of red to make a reddish-brown shade. Moisten each of the four bracts that make up the calyx and paint them one-third of the way along from the base. Leave to dry.

14 For the 4mm Bright Pink petals, make a slightly redder version of the reddish-brown mix of paint. Moisten the petals from the base then paint the lower one-third of each one. Leave to dry.

To finish

15 Complete the embroidery in the following order: work flowers 2 and 3 next, but only paint the leaves, then work flowers 4 and 5 and, again, only paint the leaves. Finish by painting the petals and bracts of each flower.

These distinctive, almost untidy looking, thistle-like flowers look so life-like when embroidered with silk ribbon in their natural colours.

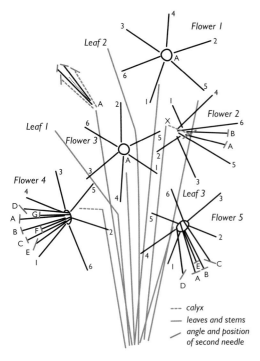

The template, half actual size; enlarge to 200 per cent. Mark each end of the petals of flowers 1 and 2 and the bud. Partly remove the template and lightly draw in the petal lines. Replace the template and transfer flowers 3, 4 and 5, using dots only to mark the positions of the trumpets. Replace the template again to mark the positions of the leaves.

--- calyx
— leaves and stems
/ angle and position of second needle

2m (79in) 13mm Pale Yellow (No. 13)

0.1m (4in) 7mm Pale Yellow (No. 13)

0.33m (13in) 13mm Yellow (No. 15)

1m (39½in) 7mm Yellow (No. 15)

0.67m (26½in) 13mm Cream (No. 156)

2.33m (92in) 7mm Cream (No. 156)

0.33m (13in) 7mm Corn (No. 35)

Narcissus

Ten minutes from where I live there is an area of woodland that, every spring, is a carpet of beautiful wild daffodils. The sun, shining through trees not yet quite ready to show their leaves, highlights the whole area. It is perfect. Daffodils are the most popular and well known of all the spring flowering bulbs. With so many varieties available, they are reliable and excellent for cutting, making them a strong favourite of gardeners and flower arrangers. The flowers, which range from miniature to large, sit singly or in clusters on strong, straight stems. They come in a broad spectrum of colours, from palest peach to deep orange, but are mostly yellow and white with trumpets the same colour.

The petals of these flowers are ribbon stitches worked using 13mm ribbon, and the trumpets are worked using either 7mm ribbon or gathered 13mm ribbon. The flowers are then lightly painted to complete the embroidery.

Painting the ribbon

1 For the leaves, cut a 1m (39½in) length of 7mm Cream ribbon. Mix yellow, blue and a spot of red silk paints to make moss green and dilute it a little. Moisten the ribbon with clean water then apply the paint randomly, leaving no bare patches. Dry and press. (See page 15.)

Flower 1

33 x 33cm (13 x 13in) linen/cotton fabric; stranded threads in Yellow (No. 305) and a white thread to match the background fabric; silk paints in navy blue, poppy red and buttercup yellow.

Flower 1

Note: when anchoring 13mm ribbon on the wrong side, stitch across the width of the ribbon to help keep the ribbon flat and wide on the right side.

4 Cut a 33cm (13in) length of 13mm Pale Yellow ribbon and work petal 1 first. Anchor the ribbon at the base of the petal and work a centre ribbon stitch at the tip. Fasten off and cut the ribbon. Work petals 2 and 3, fastening

2 Mix yellow and blue silk paint to make a blue-green, moisten the 1m (39½in) length of dyed green ribbon again with clean water and paint along one side only. Dry and press.

3 For the stem, dilute the same mix a little more and paint the remaining 1.33m (52½in) length of 7mm Cream ribbon along its length. Dry and press.

off and cutting the ribbon after each petal is worked. Now work petals 4 and 5 to sit just above the previous petals. Anchor the ribbon ready to start petal 6, but complete it later (in step 15) when the leaf behind it has been worked. Pin the end of the ribbon to one side to avoid stitching through it.

Note: detailed instructions for cutting, stitching and gathering the ribbon (steps 5 and 6) are provided on page 32.

Flower 2

5 For the frill, use 13mm Yellow ribbon and a strand of toning thread knotted at one end. Cut one end of the ribbon at an angle, then starting 1.5cm (¾in) from the cut edge, stitch a row of tiny running stitches parallel to the cut edge and along the length of the ribbon for 5cm (2in). Work back across the ribbon to the other side at the same angle, and trim off the excess 1.5cm (¾in) from the stitching. Do not anchor off or cut the thread.

6 Take the end of the ribbon through the fabric at A and anchor it. Gently pull the gathering thread to slightly curve the ribbon around the centre of the flower then anchor the other end 0.5cm (¼in) beyond the point where the ribbon came up to overlap it. Place your index finger gently in the centre, gather the ribbon to fit the circle and stab stitch it in place.

7 For the stamens, use a single strand of yellow thread and a size 24 needle. Work six stamens, as described on page 39.

Flower 2

8 Begin by working the two petals, A and B, making up the trumpet. For each stitch, anchor a length of 7mm Yellow ribbon at the base and work a straight stitch at the tip. Fasten off.

9 The six petals are all reverse centre ribbon stitches. Work them in numerical order, from 1 to 6. Use the 7mm Pale Yellow ribbon for petal 1 and 13mm Pale Yellow ribbon for petals 2 to 6.

10 For the calyx, use 7mm Corn ribbon and work a straight stitch from the top of the stem to the flower (note the angle of the second needle).

Bud

11 Using 7mm Cream ribbon, work a short straight stitch to pad the bud (see page 28). Now work the two straight stitch petals, from base to tip. Note the angle of the second needle.

12 For the calyx, use a piece of the dyed green stem ribbon and work two straight stitches to wrap around the petals.

Stems (flowers 1 and 2 and bud)

13 Cut a 20cm (7¾in) length of 7mm dyed green stem ribbon and anchor it at the top of the stem of flower 1. Carefully twist the ribbon to make a smooth, tubular stem (like a drinking straw). Take the end through to the back at the base of the stem and secure it with a thread. Cut two 17cm (6¾in)

lengths of the same ribbon to work the stems for flower 2 and the bud in the same way.

Leaves

14 Using the 7mm dyed green leaf ribbon, anchor the end at the base of leaf 1, allow the ribbon to twist once and curve, then work a centre ribbon stitch at the tip. Now work a tiny stitch over the back selvedge at the top of the fold to keep the leaf in position. Fasten off. Work leaves 2 and 3, folding them in the direction indicated on the template.

15 Complete petal 6 of flower 1, taking the needle through leaf 2.

Flower 3

16 Work as flower 1 using 13mm Cream ribbon for the petals and frill, taking care to work over the stems and leaves. Lift these petals slightly so that they sit up from the background fabric and leaves. Use a toning thread to slightly curve the stem of flower 1 behind the petals of flower 3.

Flower 4

17 Using 13mm Pale Yellow ribbon, work petals 1 to 6 in numerical order using centre ribbon stitch.

18 For the trumpet, use 7mm Yellow ribbon and work the three background petals A, B and C as straight stitches, noting the angle of the second needle. Work D next, as a right ribbon stitch, then E as a left ribbon stitch. Finish with two centre ribbon stitches for G and F, pulling the ribbon over the needle (as shown on page 29) and leaving a thin roll to form the frill. The stamens are two-loop pistil stitches worked with a strand of yellow thread (see page 36). Work the calyx as for flower 2.

Flower 5

19 Work as flower 4. For the trumpet, work straight stitches for A and B, a right ribbon stitch for D, a left ribbon stitch for C and a centre ribbon stitch for E, worked in the same way as G and F in step 18. (This flower has no stamens.)

Stems (flowers 3 to 5)

20 Cut three 12cm (4¾in) lengths of dyed green stem ribbon and work the stems of flowers 3 to 5, as described in step 13.

Painting the flowers

Note: starting with the background petals, paint alternate ones first, allow them to dry, then paint those in between. A hairdryer may be useful here.

Flower 3

Flower 4

Flower 5

By using narrower 7mm ribbon and only enlarging the template by 50 per cent, these smaller narcissi can be worked in the same way as those on the previous pages. To work miniature varieties, use the template without enlarging it at all.

21 Paint flower 3 first. Dilute a little yellow silk paint to make pale yellow, moisten the base of the frill with water then lightly add the colour to the base, allowing it to spread and fade out towards the top of the trumpet. Moisten the base of each petal and add a little colour to each.

22 For the remaining flowers, mix a little yellow and blue to make a very pale yellowy-green. Moisten one petal at a time, apply a touch of colour at the base and let the paint fade out towards the tip. Moisten and paint the base of the trumpets and the frill of flower 1. Hold the stamens upright with a pair of tweezers and paint the tips deep yellow.

The template, half actual size; enlarge to 200 per cent. Transfer the positions of the flower petals, buds, leaves and base of stem. Draw in the connecting lines of the half-open flower and buds only.

Bud 3 · Bud 5 · Bud 6 · Bud 1 · Bud 4 · Bud 2

— flower

╱ angle and position of second needle

1.33m (52½in) 13mm White (No. 03)

0.67m (26½in) 7mm White (No. 03)

0.25m (9¾in) 4mm White (No. 03)

0.67m (26½in) 13mm Moss (No. 20)

28 x 34cm (11 x 13½in) linen/cotton fabric; stranded threads in Deep Moss (No. 268), Just Green (No. 859), Soft Brown (No. 904) and a white thread to match the background fabric; silk paints in magenta, navy blue and primary yellow; fabric paints in cardinal red and buttercup yellow.

Orchid

Mystical, romantic, sculptured and flamboyant – just a few words that come to mind when describing an orchid. Every variety has its own strong, distinctive shape with almost wax-like flowers that often bloom for months on end. Add to this the vibrant colours and striking colour combinations, and this is surely one of the most spectacular of all flowers.

This particular orchid, which is just coming into flower, is a young plant that I have just been given. The petals are mainly straight stitches and a few reverse ribbon stitches, embroidered with 13mm white ribbon. The three smaller petals, bud 1 and the two petals at the back of bud 2 are worked first and painted, followed by the rest of the flower and the buds. The eye-end of a second large needle is used to shape each petal as it is worked. Take time to place each stitch, and practise painting fine vein lines on a piece of scrap ribbon first.

Preparing the background

1 Using a stiff paintbrush, apply a little gutta covering an area of approximately 0.5cm² (¼in²) over each dot marking both ends of all the petals and leaves, which is where the ribbon will go through the fabric. Leave to dry.

Flower

Note: each stitch is lifted, shaped and positioned as it is worked, then anchored off before working the next stitch. Note the angle of the second needle.

2 For the flower, cut a 25cm (9¾in) length of 13mm White ribbon and anchor it at A. Work a straight stitch at B, pulling the ribbon over the eye-end of a large needle to shape the petal. Just before completing the stitch, gently pull the ribbon over the tip of the eye-end of the needle at B to create a point. Fasten off, then work C-D and E-F.

Buds 1 and 2

3 For each of these buds, use the same ribbon and work a straight stitch for W-X. Fasten off, then work Y-Z.

Painting the petals

Note: a hairdryer is useful here; blown heat will immediately stop paint travelling.

4 Using a fine-pointed brush, mix a small amount of magenta silk paint with a touch of blue to make a deep pink-purple. Clean and dry the brush then, with a tiny amount of paint on the tip, draw in a fine vein through the centre of flower petal A-B, from the base almost to the tip. Add a few slightly curved veins either side. Paint the remaining petals of the flower and leave to dry.

5 Mix more of the same shade and dilute it to make it slightly paler. Moisten petal W-X of bud 1 with clean water and then apply paint to the middle of the petal so that it fades out towards the tip, base and sides. Add a little more paint at the base and leave to dry. Paint the second petal and bud 2, then dilute the mix to make it slightly paler and paint the three petals of the flower in the same way.

Stem

6 Make up a stem thread with eight Deep Moss and two Soft Brown strands, thread into a needle and make a knot 1cm (½in) from the end. Moisten a piece of soap with clean water and run this along the thread from the knot end. Bring the thread up at the base of the stem and, pulling it between your thumb and finger, lay it in position and take it down at 1. Do not fasten off.

7 Make another thread of four Deep Moss strands and bring this up at 2. Apply soap as before, and pull the thread through the fabric between your thumb and finger to flatten it. Take the thread over the stem at an angle and back down on the other side to couch the stem in position, then work a second stitch alongside it to complete the 'joint'. Repeat this at points 3 and 4 and fasten off both this and the stem thread.

8 Remove a Deep Moss and a Brown strand from the stem thread. Thread the remaining eight strands into a needle and knot one end. Bring the needle up to the front at 5, then remove the needle and lay the thread in position to 6. Thread a green and a brown strand into the needle, take them through to the back at 6 and work a tiny stitch over the stem at 6 to position it. Fasten off. Repeat this at 7 and 8, using the two strands taken through to the back each time to secure the stem. Fasten off the last two strands at 9. Using three strands of Just Green thread (soaped), work stems 10, 11 and 12. Fasten off. Do not couch the stems in place.

Completing bud 2

9 Anchor a length of 13mm White ribbon at U and work a reverse centre ribbon stitch at V, taking care to position this petal over the first petals. Fasten off.

Completing the flower

10 Anchor a length of 13mm White ribbon at G and work a straight stitch at H, using a second needle to lift the ribbon and curve the outside edge. Keep the edge that will lie in the centre of the petal straight. Fasten off. Anchor the ribbon at I and repeat for I-J, using the second needle to sit the ribbon in line with G-H and curve the outer edge as before to create a single petal. Fasten off. Work straight stitches K-L and M-N in the same way.

11 Anchor the ribbon at O and, lifting the ribbon with a second needle, work a centre ribbon stitch at P. Fasten off.

12 Thread the 4mm White ribbon into a needle, knot one end and bring the needle up at O. Using a second needle to control the ribbon, work a straight stitch at Q, the same height as O-P. Bring the needle up again just above Q and work a loose two-loop French knot. Fasten off.

13 Anchor the 7mm White ribbon just to the left of O. Place it so that a selvedge sits along the curved line marked on the template to the left of O-Q. Work a curved right ribbon stitch, with the selvedge still touching the fabric. Fasten off. Work a left ribbon stitch in the same way just to the right of O-Q.

Buds 3 to 6

14 Using 7mm White ribbon, work straight stitches for the two outer petals of bud 3, fastening off after each one. Work a reverse ribbon stitch for the centre petal and fasten off. Work the two petals of bud 4 as straight stitches that overlap, again fastening off after each one.

15 Buds 5 and 6 are single straight stitches, using a second needle at the base to pull the ribbon over and elongate the tips. Fasten off each bud as it is worked.

Leaves

16 Each leaf consists of two stitches. Using 13mm Moss ribbon, anchor one end at the base of leaf 1 (A) and work a straight stitch at B. Fasten off. Anchor the ribbon at C and work a left ribbon stitch at D. For leaves 2 and 3, work a straight stitch for A-B, and a right ribbon stitch for C-D for leaf 2 and a left ribbon stitch for C-D for leaf 3.

Completing the painting

Note: it is important to retain the shapes and positions of the petals and leaves as they are painted. However, if necessary a petal can be remoistened and a small piece of wadding placed underneath to pad it out and reshape it while the ribbon dries (see page 41).

17 Paint in the veins on the petals of bud 2 following the instructions in step 4. Leave to dry. Dilute the paint to make it a little paler, moisten petals G-H and I-J and apply paint in the centre of each one so that the colour fades out completely at the edges and at the top. Paint petals K-L and M-N in the same way and leave to dry. Moisten the base of the French knot and touch the base only with paint, leaving a white top. Leave to dry.

18 Mix a little of the darker tone and use it to deepen the colour near the base of the two large flower petals (use the picture for reference). Leave to dry. Moisten petal R-S and paint the lower edge nearest the fabric so that it fades out towards the top edge. Paint petal T-U on the opposite side in the same way. Paint the top petal of bud 2.

19 Dilute the paint to make it paler, moisten buds 3 and 4 and just colour the tips of each petal. Leave to dry.

20 Using yellow fabric paint and a fine brush, paint the 4mm stitch O-Q in the centre of the flower. Leave to dry, then mix a tiny spot of blue silk paint with red fabric paint to make a browny red and, using a clean, dry brush, paint tiny dots over the yellow. Leave to dry.

21 Mix yellow and blue silk paint to make a deep green, moisten one of the leaves 0.5cm (¼in) from each end and paint along both outside edges, allowing the colour to blend and fade out towards the centre. Paint the other leaves in the same way.

22 Dilute the green paint a little, moisten bud 3 and paint from the stem end to leave a pale pink tip. Repeat for bud 4, and paint buds 5 and 6 green only to complete.

These three orchids are embroidered using the same basic techniques but with slight variations. The centres of the green and the pale pink orchid are both worked with 13mm ribbon, but each petal of the pink variety is a single 13mm stitch whereas the petals of the green flower are each worked as two stitches. The red orchid at the bottom has the same types of petals as the pink flower above it, but two 13mm stitches are worked for the wider centre.

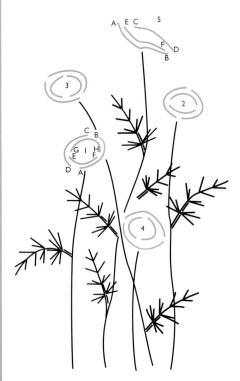

The template, half actual size; enlarge to 200 per cent. Transfer the positions of the petals, leaves and the base of the stem. Lightly draw in the curved lines marked on the template for the petals and the centre line for the leaves.

1.75m (69in) 13mm White (No. 03)

3m (118½in) 2mm Just Green (No. 31)

28 x 34cm (11 x 13½in) linen/cotton fabric; 20 x 20cm (7¾ x 7¾in) silk habitai; 10 x 10cm (4 x 4in) stiff interfacing; stranded threads in Pale Pink (No. 73), Pale Yellow (No. 292), Yellow (No. 305), Soft Apple Green (No. 264), Just Green (No. 859) and a white thread to match the background fabric; silk paints in poppy red, magenta, navy blue and primary yellow; fabric paints in cobalt blue, buttercup yellow and white; 75cm (29½in) kitchen string; small piece of wadding.

Papaver

These delicate flowers, with their tissue-like petals, are a cultivated form of the field or corn poppy. They can be found growing wild in many parts of the world. Their colours range from white through yellow and orange to red, and en masse, moving gently in the breeze, they are a spectacular sight. The cultivated, hardy perennial varieties for the flower garden are attractive at every stage. Big fat buds develop into magnificent flowers, followed by large seed heads, often dried for decoration.

Lengths of gathered ribbon have been stitched to shape the petals so that the flowers appear to tilt or face in different directions. When the embroidery is complete, the petals are moistened and the edges painted delicate shades in various tones of red and pink.

Stitching the ribbon

Note: do not cut the 13mm ribbon until the running stitches have been worked.

1 Thread a fine needle with a strand of Pale Pink thread and knot one end. Cut one end of the 13mm White ribbon at an angle. Starting 1.5cm (¾in) from the cut end, follow steps 1 to 4 on page 32, working a 6cm (2¼in) line of tiny running stitches. Do not fasten off or cut the thread, but cut the ribbon at an angle, 1.5cm (¾in) from the stitch line.

2 Work seven more lengths with 6cm (2¼in) of stitching, four with 5cm (2in) and seven lengths with 4cm (1½in) of stitching. Use a fine pencil to mark the length of each piece of ribbon on the tag end.

Flowers

Note: take care not to stitch through any gathering stitches while you work the petals.

3 Referring to pages 32–33, use a white thread to anchor the knot end of a 6cm (2¼in) length of ribbon at A of flower 1, slightly gather the ribbon, then take the other end through at B. Secure this end with the white thread, then bring the thread through to the front at A.

4 Pull the pink gathering thread so that the ribbon fits along the line A-B, then use the white thread to work tiny stitches over the gathering

line to secure the petal. Fasten off. Gently pull the gathering thread to seat the petal and fasten it off. Now work C-D using a 6cm (2¼in) length, E-F using 5cm (2in) and G-H using a 4cm (1½in) length of ribbon.

5 Work flower 2 in the same way. For flowers 3 and 4, use 4cm (1½in) lengths for both E-F and G-H.

6 For flower 5, use 5cm (2in) ribbons for A-B and C-D and 4cm (1½in) ribbon for E-F. Stitch the ribbon to the fabric along the lower edge so that it sits up from the fabric.

Painting the petals

Note: test each colour shade on a spare piece of silk before painting the petals.

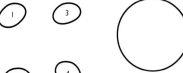

Templates for the centres of flowers 1 to 4; enlarge to 200 per cent. (Use the four smaller templates for the interfacing, and the larger template on the right for the silk.)

To paint the flowers, mix the colour first then, holding the ribbon away from the fabric (see page 17), moisten a petal with clean water. Using a clean, pointed paintbrush apply the paint round the selvedge only, allowing the colour to fade down towards the centre. Repeat this step to add more colour to the petal then leave to dry. More colour can be added later if necessary.

7 Starting with flower 3, mix a little magenta silk paint with water to make a very pale tone. Moisten a petal with clean water and paint a line around the selvedge. Leave to dry. Paint the rest of the petals.

Note: using a hairdryer will speed up drying and stop the colour from spreading too far.

8 Paint the remaining flowers in the same way. For flower 5 use a paler version of the same mix, and for flower 1 add a little red to the magenta to make a deeper tone and paint it twice. Flower 2 is painted three times using a mix of red and magenta diluted a little. For flower 4 use the same mix with just a touch of blue added and paint it four times.

Flower centres

Work each flower centre following the steps for flower 1 below. Note that all of the flower centres vary slightly in shape.

9 Put the silk in a hoop, mix blue and yellow silk paints to make pale green, then paint the silk. Dry and press.

10 For each flower, use the templates to cut out a circle from the green silk and a disc from the interfacing and wadding.

Note: refer to the instructions on page 40 for making the centres of the poppies.

11 Thread a fine needle with a 50cm (19¾in) strand of Soft Apple Green thread and make a knot 2cm (¾in) from one end. Make a narrow hem around the edge of the silk for flower 1 using tiny running stitches. Do not cut this thread.

12 Thread another needle with a strand of Soft Apple Green thread and knot one end. Place the silk face down on a foam pad so that the hem is uppermost, then place the interfacing disc for flower 1 in the centre and the wadding

on top. Take the needle down through the centre of the three layers, then bring it back up close to, but not through, the same hole. Remove the needle but do not cut the thread.

13 Gently pull each end of the gathering thread around the hem of the silk so that it sits evenly and smoothly around the interfacing and covers the wadding. Tie the

ends together securely and cut the threads.

14 Take the first thread through the silk to just below the edge of the disc. Work small running stitches around just under the edge of the disc. Pull the thread carefully, easing the fabric under the disc to make a smooth ridge. Secure the thread but do not cut it.

15 Take the thread across the centre of the disc and secure it on the underside but do not cut it. Work another stitch across at 90° to the first, then work a tiny stitch over the point where they cross to keep the threads in place. Work two more stitches to evenly divide the surface into eight segments. Fasten the thread off securely.

16 Using the same coloured thread, bring it up through the layers to the centre of the disc and work a two-loop French knot. Bring the needle back up on the edge of the disc, underneath one of the stitches that cross the centre. Take the needle under the next stitch along so that the working thread lies exactly on the edge of the disc. Take the needle back over and under the stitch through a tiny piece of silk to secure the thread and work the edge of the next segment in the same way. Repeat all the way round the disc, secure the thread then take it back to the centre of the base ready to secure it in the centre of a flower in step 15.

17 Place the disc in the centre of flower 1 and secure it with the thread so that it sits closer to the fabric along the back edge (use the picture for guidance). This gives the flower a three-dimensional appearance.

18 Work the stamens as described on page 37 using a strand each of both yellow threads.

Stems

19 Make a blue-green mix with blue and yellow fabric paint and add white to make it paler and duller. Lay the length of string on a sheet of scrap paper and paint it all over. Leave to dry.

20 Referring to the template and using the Just Green thread, oversew one end of the string in position under flower 3. Cut the string at the base and repeat for flowers 1 and 4. Oversew at the base of each stem to secure, fastening off and cutting the thread each time.

21 Work the stem of flower 5 in the same way, but cut the string where it goes behind flower 4 (as shown on the template) to keep the stem flat. Work the stem of flower 2.

Leaves

Work each leaf following step 23 and referring to the diagram below. Note that some leaves lie under a stem; others over a stem.

22 Mix a blue-green with yellow and blue silk paint, moisten the 2mm Just Green ribbon and dye it randomly (see page 15). Dry and press.

23 Cut a 45cm (17¾in) length of the dyed green ribbon, thread it into a size 24 needle and knot one end. Bring the needle up at A, down at B, up again at C then, leaving the stitch loose, take the needle down at D. Bring the needle up again at B and tighten the ribbon to complete a fly stitch, C-D-E. Bring the needle up at E and continue to X at the base of the leaf. Now work back up from X, working straight stitches in between the fly stitches, using the template for guidance. Fasten off.

To finish

24 Lift the petals as indicated in the picture to give shape to each flower. A hairdryer is useful here – use clean water to moisten the petals, then use the hairdryer to blow heat on to the ribbon and push it into the required position.

A red poppy is such a recognisable, flamboyant, flower. To work this poppy I have enlarged the centre of the flower to 175 per cent. Two strands of black thread are used to cover the green silk base as before, then the thread is woven around the threads in the middle to form a dense, black centre. An extra gathered length of red ribbon is worked, and placed across and below the lower petal. Two straight stitch leaves are worked with green ribbon, and the bud is attached so that it touches the fabric at the back and sits up away from the fabric at the front. Green garden string is used for the stem.

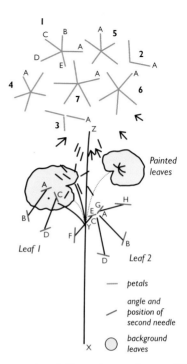

The template, half actual size; enlarge to 200 per cent. Transfer points X, Y and Z of the stem and both ends of the petals and leaves. Place light dots around the background leaves. Remove the template and lightly draw in the connecting lines of the petals, buds and leaves (but not those of the background leaves).

1.75cm (69in) 13mm Just Pink (No. 05)

0.5m (19¾in) 4mm Just Pink (No. 05)

1m (39½in) 13mm Just Green (No. 31)

0.5m (19¾in) 4mm Just Green (No. 31)

0.75m (29½in) 2mm Just Green (No. 31)

28 x 33cm (11 x 13in) linen/cotton fabric; stranded threads in Moss (No. 266), Soft Apple Green (No. 264), Sand (No. 854) and a white thread to match the background fabric; silk paints in magenta, poppy red, navy blue and primary yellow; fabric paints in primary yellow and white.

Pelargonium

Commonly called geraniums, these pretty flowers can be found growing in pots, window boxes, flower borders and formal flower beds in towns and cities throughout the world. Grown for their large blooms, each is made up of a number of small flowers, creating huge splashes of vibrant colour that sit above interesting, aromatic foliage. Their colours can be bright and bold or pale and delicate, and shaded with either a deep centre or a very pale centre, as I have chosen here. The leaves are often two toned, frequently with splashes of red.

The background leaves are painted on to the fabric, giving the embroidery depth. For the flowers I have worked straight stitch petals using 13mm ribbon, which I have then painted.

Painting the background

1 Mix yellow fabric paint with a touch of blue silk paint to make a moss green. Using a clean, dry, stiff brush and little paint, lightly paint from the outside edge of each leaf to the centre, just covering the pencil dots. Dilute a spot of red to make it very pale and, referring to the picture, use the pointed brush to apply a dab of colour to each section of the leaves, 0.5cm (¼in) from the outer edge. Make the green mix a little darker and lightly paint in the veins and both stems. Leave to dry.

Painting the ribbons for the leaves and the thread

2 Mix yellow and blue silk paint to make two greens then add a touch of red to make a slightly browner tone. Moisten the 2,4 and 13mm Just Green ribbons with water and dye them randomly (see page 15). Leave them to dry then press.

3 Moisten and dye the Soft Apple Green thread the same way.

Flowers

Note: using 20cm (7¾in) lengths of ribbon, work the flowers in numerical order. The petals of flowers 1 and 3 are towards the back of the picture and lie almost flat, as does petal A of the remaining flowers. All the other petals are fuller.

4 Pass a large needle through the fabric at the centre of flower 1 to make a hole. Using a size 13 needle, take a short end of the 13mm Just Pink ribbon through to the back of the fabric at the tip of petal A. Ease the ribbon back and forth through the fabric until the edges of the ribbon turn downwards when in position. Anchor the ribbon (see page 23), then take the needle and thread to one side ready to use later.

5 On the right side of the fabric, re-thread the ribbon into a size 13 needle and work a straight stitch at the centre of the flower, taking the needle through the same hole and pulling the ribbon over the eye-end of a second large needle placed at the tip of the petal (see page 27). Bring the needle up at the tip of petal B, work four more petals and fasten off.

6 Work flowers 2 to 5 in the same way.

Stem

7 Make up a stem thread with five strands of Moss, three strands of dyed green and three of Sand, thread it into a needle and knot one end. Moisten and soap the thread and bring it up at X. Pull it over a second needle to flatten it to Y and use a single dyed thread to secure it at Y. Do not flatten the rest of the stem to make it a little narrower and secure it with a few stitches at Z.

8 Use three strands at a time, soaped, to work a curved stem to each flower and bud. Use the eye-end of the needle to pass the stems behind the petals where necessary.

Painting flower 1 and the ribbon for the buds

Note: a hairdryer will speed up drying time and prevent any colour seeping into another petal or the background fabric.

9 Make two mixes of magenta silk paint with a little red and just a touch of blue, then dilute each one to make a slightly pale and a very pale mix. Test the colours on a spare piece of ribbon.

10 Place a small foam pad behind flower 1 and use glass-headed pins to hold the petals not being painted out of the way (see page 17). Using a clean brush, moisten each petal with water then apply the palest shade in a curved line 0.5cm (¼in) from the tip across the fullest part of petal A. The paint should fade out towards the centre of the petal. Before it has dried, paint a thin line across the same curve with the deeper tone to shade the petal more deeply. Paint the remaining petals and leave to dry, then paint the rest of the flowers.

11 Dye the 4mm Just Pink ribbon randomly in the paint that is left from step 10 (the deeper of the two mixes). Dry and press.

12 Mix a little red, blue and yellow silk paint to make a brown-green shade, do not dilute, and apply a tiny spot at the centre of each flower.

Buds

13 Using the 4mm dyed pink ribbon work small straight stitches from the base to the tip of each bud. Fasten off as each petal is worked.

14 Use the 2mm dyed green ribbon to work a tiny straight stitch either side of each bud for the calyx and three for both half flowers (flowers 2 and 3). Now use the 4mm dyed green ribbon and work all the small green buds.

Leaves

15 Using the 13mm dyed green ribbon, note the angle of the second large needle and work the straight stitch A-B followed by C-D of leaf 1. Anchor off after each stitch is worked. Using a single strand of dyed thread, work a tiny stitch through both the edges at W to pull both ribbons down to shape the leaf.

16 Using white fabric paint and a fine-pointed brush, paint fine veins radiating out half way to the edge from W.

17 Work leaf 2 in the order indicated on the template. Moisten leaves 1 and 2, dilute a little red silk paint and paint in small red areas on each part of each leaf, 0.5cm (¼in) from the edge of the leaf (as in the picture).

18 Make a stem thread with two strands of Sand and two of Soft Apple Green, soap the thread, then work a stem from Y to W under leaf 1 and repeat for leaf 2. Use one strand of each colour to work a curved stem to each bud.

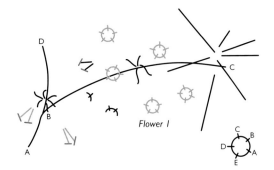

Flower I

The template, half actual size; enlarge to 200 per cent. Mark dots along the length of the branch, each end of the main leaves and around the flower centre circles. Remove the template and lightly draw in the branch and the flower centres (including the five short intersecting lines). For the leaves, draw in a short line only starting from the end nearest the stem (this is to show the direction of the stitches).

2m (79in) 13mm White (No. 03)

0.5m (19¾in) 7mm White (No. 03)

0.5m (19¾in) 13mm Moss (No. 20)

0.33m (13in) 7mm Moss (No. 20)

0.33cm (13in) 4mm Moss (No. 20)

33 x 33cm (13 x 13in) linen/cotton fabric; stranded threads in Pale Pink (No. 73), Pale Yellow (No. 292), Donkey (No. 393) and a white thread to match the background fabric; silk paints in magenta, raspberry, navy blue and primary yellow; fabric paints in primary yellow, white and poppy red; 50cm (19¾in) undyed garden string.

Prunus

Japanese cherry blossom flowers mainly in the spring and loves full sun – explosions of pale pink blossom against a clear blue sky signal the end of winter and is quite magical. A similar method to that described here could be used for plum, almond and peach blossoms. The colours of these blossoms vary from white through pink to almost red, and the flowers may be single or double and may sit a little differently on the branch or twig, but very little alteration would be needed for any one of these.

Garden string is used for the branch, untwisted to make it slightly rough and hairy, and the ribbon has been shaded before stitching. The upright stamens with their orange tips complete the blossoms, and the red-tinted leaves add colour and depth to the embroidery.

Painting the ribbon

Note: the paint colour will appear a lot deeper once the ribbon is gathered.

1 For the flowers, mix a little raspberry with some magenta silk paint and dilute it to make a very pale mix. Test the colour on a piece of spare ribbon. Secure the end of the 13mm White ribbon at one end (see page 15) and use a stiff brush to wet the entire length. Use a medium-sized brush to paint along one edge only – do not worry if this line is uneven. Suspend the ribbon to dry.

2 Make the colour slightly deeper and paint the 7mm White ribbon very randomly (see page 15). Dry then press both ribbons.

3 Dye the ribbons for the leaves using dilute magenta silk paint. Moisten all three Moss ribbons and dye them randomly, leaving many areas free of paint. Suspend the ribbons to dry and press.

Main branch

Note: use soap to help form the stem and keep its shape (see page 39).

4 Cut the string in half and untwist both halves to separate the strands. Put the strands back together, untwisted, and dampen. Pull the string between your fingers to reshape it, remove any excess water with a tissue, then pull the soap along the length of the string several times. Lay the string along A-C, cut each end at an angle and couch it in place using a few stitches worked with the Donkey thread. Using four strands of string only, soap and then position the stem B-D. Cut the ends at an angle and couch the stem in place as before.

Flowers

Note: only cut the 13mm ribbon after the running stitches of each piece have been stitched.

In step 5, it is important to work the stitches along the pink selvedge and across to the white selvedge, then take a single straight stitch back to the pink selvedge. This stitch will encourage the petal to tip forwards when it is attached to the fabric.

5 Thread the Pale Pink thread into a fine needle and knot one end. Referring to page 32, work tiny running stitches along the dyed pink ribbon as shown in the diagram at the bottom of the page, then cut the ribbon at an angle 1cm (½in) from the last line of stitching. Do not cut the thread or fasten off. Work four more identical lengths.

6 Work two further lengths of ribbon for the partly open flowers – one consisting of three sections of 2.5cm (1in) lines of stitching, and one consisting of two sections of 2cm (¾in) lines of stitching.

7 Take one of the longer lengths of dyed pink ribbon (those made in step 5). Referring to page 33, use a white thread to anchor the knot end of the ribbon at A of flower 1. Without gathering the ribbon, bring the needle up at B and work a stitch over the selvedge between the first two sections of stitching. Let the petal fold outwards. Repeat for the next four sections, then take the end of the ribbon carefully through the same hole at A to complete the circle. Fasten off behind the petal (not behind the centre of the flower).

8 Place your index finger in the centre of the flower and gently pull the gathering thread to form the petals and sit them evenly around the centre circle. Use this thread to stitch them

neatly in place. Ease the edges of the petals forwards, and if needed work a single stitch through the edge of any petal that may be twisted to place it in position. Fasten off both ends of the gathering thread.

9 Work the remaining flowers and the partly open flowers in the same way, using appropriate lengths of ribbon.

Buds

10 Each bud consists of two straight stitches worked from the base to the tip in 7mm dyed pink ribbon. Pull the ribbon over a second needle to create the bulbous tip (see page 26).

Flower stems

11 Using one strand of string, moisten and soap as before, then take an end through to the back and secure it with a thread. Work a loose, curving straight stitch from the main branch to flower 1 and secure it at the back. Work the stems to the remaining flowers and buds.

Leaves

12 Work the small leaves at the base of the bud and flower stems in ribbon stitch using 4mm dyed green ribbon.

13 Use 13mm dyed green ribbon for the three large leaves at the end of the branch, and 7mm for all the others. Work a loose straight stitch to connect each of these leaves to the branch using three strands of Donkey thread.

Flower centres

14 The stamens consist of a strand each of white and Pale Yellow thread. Wax the thread, work three loops in the centre of flower 1 and fasten off. Cut them to length 0.5cm (¼in). Work a length of six to eight two- and three-loop French knots (see page 39) and attach them between the stamens already worked.

15 Mix a little white and red fabric paint with a touch of yellow silk paint to make orange, then with a fine paintbrush carefully paint the tip of each stamen.

Painting the stems and leaves

16 Mix a little blue silk paint with a touch of yellow and red fabric paint to make a brown-green, then lightly paint along the length of the string branches and stems.

17 Using the same mix and the tip of a fine brush, paint a fine centre vein that fades away towards the tip along each leaf. Add the short, curved side veins to complete the embroidery.

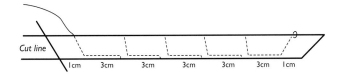

Cut line   1cm   3cm   3cm   3cm   3cm   3cm   1cm

Stitching the ribbon for the flowers.

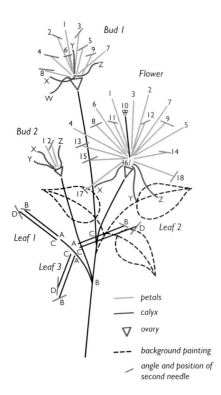

- —— petals
- —— calyx
- ▽ ovary
- --- background painting
- ╱ angle and position of second needle

The template, half actual size; enlarge to 200 per cent. Begin by marking the outlines of the painted background leaves, the centre vein lines and the stem from B only using light dots made with a sharp pencil. Remove the template and paint the background leaves. Replace the template accurately and mark the base and tip of each flower petal except for petals 8, 9 and 10; all the petals except for petal 4 of bud 1; all the petals and the calyx of bud 2; each end of the leaves; the base of stem A; and the points where the side stems join the main stem at B and C.

2m (79in) 13mm Cream (No. 156)

0.67m (26½in) 13mm Moss (No. 20)

0.67m (26½in) 7mm Moss (No. 20)

30 x 40cm (11¾ x 15¾in) linen/cotton fabric; stranded threads in Deep Moss (No. 268), Moss (No. 266) and a white thread to match the background fabric; silk paints in magenta, navy blue, poppy red and primary yellow; fabric paints in navy blue, cardinal red and buttercup yellow.

Rosa

Roses have been grown for centuries all over the world. In earlier times the rose was used for medicinal purposes and in religious ceremonies as a symbol of earthly and heavenly perfection. More recently it has become a symbol of purity and love.

There is a rose for every situation, from miniature plants to shrubs of all sizes, including climbers that flower from early summer through to the first frosts of autumn. Often with thorny stems, the flowers may be single or clustered and vary greatly in colour, size and form.

Cream 13mm ribbon has been used to embroider the petals, and the eye-end of a large needle is used to shape and position each petal. The tip of the eye-end of the second needle (or a cotton bud) is used to form the point of the straight stitch petals at the back of the flower. Each petal is then lightly shaded and the leaves painted to complete the rose.

Painting the background leaves

Note: make the painted leaves slightly larger than those marked on the template to cover the pencil dots.

1 Using fabric paint, mix blue and yellow to make green. Add a spot of red to half the mix to make a different shade, and dilute it with just a little water to make it paler.

2 Using both mixes and a clean, pointed paintbrush and just a little paint, start at the base of a leaf and paint a fine centre vein almost to the tip. With a stiff brush, use curved brushstrokes to lightly paint one half of the leaf from the vein to the edge, just covering the

dots. Paint the other side in the same way, then complete the other two leaves.

3 Add a little red to one of the mixes to make a browner green and paint in the stems from the base to part way along the centre vein. Add a touch more red and paint a fine, broken line around the edge of each leaf (see picture). Dry and press the fabric.

Bud 1

Note: when stitching the buds and the flower, if the position of a petal is hidden by a petal already worked, either carefully lift the petal to see underneath or refer to the template and picture.

4 Thread a short length of 13mm Cream ribbon into a size 13 needle and secure it at the base of petal 1, behind the petal about to be worked. Re-thread the needle and work a straight stitch at the tip, pulling the ribbon over the tip of the eye-end of second needle to shape the petal (see page 27). Fasten off.

Note: when fastening off a stitch, do not cut the thread, but instead take it to one side and wind it around the needle to tension it, ready to anchor the next petal.

5 Work the remaining petals as follows: petal 2 – left ribbon stitch; petal 3 – right ribbon stitch; petals 4 and 5 – straight stitches; petal 6 – centre ribbon stitch; and petals 7–9 straight stitches.

Flower

6 Work petals 1–9 as straight stitches. Next bring the needle up at the base of petal 10 and work a loose three-loop French knot, making the second loop slightly looser than the first and the third loop slightly looser still. Position the knot as the needle is taken through to the back at 10 and fasten off. With a toning thread, work a stitch through the base of the knot to hold it in position.

7 Petals 11 and 12 are centre ribbon stitches; petals 13–15 are straight stitches and petal 16 is a looped ribbon stitch (see page 31). For petals 17 and 18, work straight stitches, first placing a cotton bud at the base of the each petal to create a bowl shape, then using a second needle to shape the ribbon for the petal.

Bud 2

8 Work a straight stitch for petal 1. Use the tip of the eye-end of a second needle to form a point, and roll the sides of the ribbon under to shape and narrow the stitch. For petal 2, work a right ribbon stitch.

Painting the flower and buds

Note: paint the petals in numerical order. Place a foam pad under the rose and use glass-headed pins to hold the petals away from those being painted (see page 17). Take care not to place a pin through a petal where the pin mark may show.

9 Mix magenta with a little red and yellow silk paint, and dilute with water to the required tone. Test the colour on a spare piece of ribbon and mix sufficient paint to fill a teaspoon.

10 Starting with petal 1 of the flower, moisten the visible area with clean water, stopping just short of the tip. Pick up a little paint with the end of a brush and just touch the petal 0.5cm (¼in) from the tip. Apply a touch more paint if needed, taking care not to make the ribbon too wet. Leave to dry.

11 Continue to paint the petals in order; paint the French knot after petal 9, applying paint just below the top rolled edges and allowing it to fade out.

12 Paint the buds in the same way, but make petal 1 of bud 2 slightly deeper in tone.

13 Make a very pale mix of yellow silk paint. Moisten the base of flower petal 11 and just touch it with a little paint on the tip of a brush. Leave to dry. Shade the base of every petal that is visible in the same way.

Calyxes

Note: all the calyxes are worked in double ribbon stitch, apart from the stitch at W.

14 Begin with bud 1. Anchor a length of 7mm Moss ribbon at the base of W and work a reverse ribbon stitch at the tip, pulling the ribbon over a second needle to elongate the stitch (see page 26). Fasten off. Work a left ribbon stitch for X, a centre ribbon stitch for Y and a right ribbon stitch for Z. In each case, pull the ribbon to elongate the tip while at the same time taking care to sit the ribbon round the shape of the bud. For the ovary at the bottom of the calyx, work a straight stitch from the base, pulling the ribbon over the eye-end of a second needle placed close to the bud.

15 For bud 2, work left ribbon stitches for X and Y and a right ribbon stitch for Z. Work the ovary as for bud 1.

16 The flower has a left ribbon stitch for X, a centre ribbon stitch for Y and a right ribbon stitch for Z. The ovary is worked as above.

Flower stems

17 Make up a stem thread with five Deep Moss and two Moss strands, thread it into a needle and make a knot 2cm (¾in) from one end. Rub a moist piece of soap along the thread from the knot end. Bring the needle up at the base of the stem at A and take it down at the base of the flower. Use a toning thread to work a stitch at B to position it. Fasten off all the threads.

18 Make up a thread of one Moss and three Deep Moss strands to work the stems of both buds. Work them from C and B for buds 1 and 2 respectively. Use the eye-end of the needle to pass the thread behind the petals of the flower, fastening off as each is worked.

Leaves

19 Anchor a length of 13mm Moss ribbon at A of leaf 1, work a straight stitch at B and fasten off. Anchor the ribbon at C and work a right ribbon stitch at D. Fasten off.

20 For leaves 2 and 3, work A-B as a straight stitch and C-D as a left ribbon stitch.

21 Work a stem from B to the base of leaf 1, as for the stems to the buds (see step 18).

Painting the leaves

22 Starting with leaf 1, mix blue silk paint and yellow fabric paint to make a deep green. Do not dilute the mix and do not moisten the ribbon. Use the point of a fine brush to paint in the centre vein then the fine side veins, taking them not quite to the edge of the leaf. Leave to dry. Dilute the paint a little, moisten the leaf then lightly shade some areas to complete. Paint leaves 1 and 2 in the same way.

There are many different types of rose in myriad colours, from miniature varieties to large, intricate blooms, and from those with just five petals, such as the delicate, single briar rose (top right), to those with many densely packed petals. The top four roses are worked with 13mm ribbon and the petals are then shaded at either their base or their tip. The cluster of small pink roses consist of looped ribbon stitches worked with 7mm pink ribbon. They have not been painted.

Painting the calyxes

23 Use the same mix as in step 22, and do not moisten the ribbon. Starting with bud 1, and using a second needle to lift the ribbon, paint each stitch leaving the centre area free of paint to suggest light and shade. Paint the ovary below the bud in the same way. Paint the other two calyxes and leave to dry.

Note: 13mm ribbon is particularly vulnerable to seepage; see pages 14 and 17.

Thorns

24 Thread two strands of Deep Moss into a fine needle and, referring to the picture, work a tiny lazy daisy stitch over the stem from right to left, just up from the base, to make a thorn. Fasten off. Repeat on the right of the stem at B and part of the way up the stem of bud 2.

This spray of roses is a similar to that on page 103, though it is a little smaller and has fewer petals. It is worked with 13mm Just Pink (No. 05) ribbon, then the petals are delicately shaded in the bowl, from the base of each petal. When dry, the base of the visible petals are tinted a very pale green.

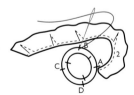

The template, half actual size; enlarge to 200 per cent. Make dots around the flower circles and mark points A–D on each, and also mark the top and bottom of each stem, the calyx of the bud and the positions of the leaves. Lightly draw in the circles.

1.5m (59¼in) 13mm White (No. 03)

1.5m (59¼in) 4mm Soft Green (No. 33)

Stitching the petals.

35 x 28cm (13¾ x 11in) linen/cotton fabric; stranded threads in Green (No. 216), Just Green (No. 859), Soft Apple Green (No. 264), Pale Blue (No. 144) and a white thread to match the background fabric; silk paints in navy blue and primary yellow; fabric paints in cobalt blue and buttercup yellow.

Scabiosa

The wild scabious is a small flower, found growing in dry meadows throughout Europe, the Mediterranean and many other parts of the world. Here I have chosen to embroider the cultivated variety, with its large, pin-cushion centre surrounded with delicately frilled petals. The soft whites, pale yellows, pinks and blues of this flower, with its long, straight stems, makes it a very pretty flower in every sense, popular with gardeners and flower arrangers alike.

For the petals, two lengths of gathered 13mm white ribbon are worked first, then the centre is filled with French knots and the petals shaded blue from the selvedge.

Stitching the ribbon

Note: do not cut the 13mm ribbon until the running stitches have been worked.

1 Thread a fine needle with a Pale Blue thread, but do not knot the end. Referring to pages 32–33 and following carefully the diagram at the bottom of the page, bring the needle through at A on the 13mm White ribbon and, leaving a 10cm (4in) tail thread, work tiny running stitches across the ribbon at an angle, along the selvedge for 3cm (1¼in), then three-quarters of the way back across the ribbon at a slight angle. Work a single straight stitch on the front of the ribbon back to the selvedge and continue along to E. Do not fasten off or cut the thread. Cut off the ribbon at an angle, 1.5cm (¾in) from the last line of stitching.

2 Stitch three more lengths of ribbon: one as in step 1, and two with six 2.5cm (1in) sections.

Flowers

Note: refer to pages 32–33 for gathering techniques.

3 Using a white thread, anchor the knot end of one of the longer pieces of ribbon at A of flower 1, then bring the needle up at B (see the diagram on the left). Gather the ribbon slightly and lay it along the marked line to B. Anchor the ribbon at B with a tiny stitch placed at point B on the ribbon, avoiding the gathering thread.

4 Bring the needle up at C and repeat, anchoring point C on the ribbon at C on the fabric, and point D on the ribbon at D on the fabric. Now take the tag end down at A, so that both ends of the petal meet and, without stitching through the gathering stitches, secure with the white thread. Bring the thread up through at A, just inside the centre of the flower.

5 Lightly place your fingers over the frill and at the same time gently pull each end of the

gathering thread to fit the edge of the ribbon to the drawn petal line and shape the petals. Do not cut the gathering threads – twist them around a pin to secure them to one side of the embroidery.

6 Even out each gathered section if needed, then use the anchor thread to stitch over the gathering line to secure each section. Gently pull each end of the gathering thread again to seat the petals and anchor all the threads.

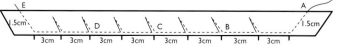

Stitching the ribbon for the flowers.

7 Use one of the shorter lengths of ribbon to work the inner petals in the same way.

8 Work flower 2 as flower 1.

Painting the petals

Note: work on a foam pad and use glass-headed pins inserted through the fabric (not the ribbon) to hold the inner petals away from the outer petals as they are painted (see page 17).

9 For flower 1, mix a little yellow and blue silk paint to make a pale green, moisten the outer petals with clean water and paint a fine line around the base to just colour them.

10 While the petals are still damp, dilute some blue silk paint, test it on a piece of scrap ribbon and use a clean, dry brush to apply paint around the top selvedge. Repeat once more, allowing the colour to fade towards the flower centre. Repeat if more colour is needed.

11 Paint the inner petals in the same way.

12 Paint flower 2 in the same way as flower 1.

Flower centres

13 Make up a thread of one Pale Blue, one Soft Apple Green and two Just Green strands, thread it into a size 24 needle and knot one end. Place a three-loop French knot in the centre of flower 1, work a tight ring of three-loop French knots around it, then fill the rest of the flower centre with tightly packed two-loop French knots.

14 Work flower 2 as flower 1.

Bud

15 Work the French knot centre as for the flowers, then use the 4mm Soft Green ribbon to work ribbon stitches radiating out from the French knots for the calyx.

Stems

16 Make up a thread with four strands of Green and four of Just Green. Thread it into a needle and make a knot 10cm (4in) from one end. For each flower, work a straight stitch from the base of the stem and fasten off behind the flower. Remove one strand of each colour and work the bud stem, then couch each stem in place with a toning thread.

Leaves

17 Using 4mm Soft Green ribbon, work the long, centre ribbon stitches first then the smaller side leaves. Fasten off.

18 Mix yellow and blue fabric paint to make green, then use a fine brush to paint a central vein through each leaf and the sepals of the calyx.

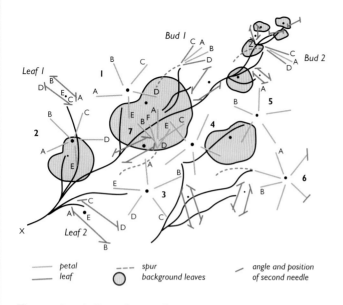

—— petal   - - - spur   ╱ angle and position
—— leaf   🟢 background leaves   of second needle

Tropaeolum

From mid- through to early summer the large, bold trumpet-shaped flowers of the nasturtium can be found winding up and through anything they come into contact with. Sitting above flat, saucer-shaped leaves, flowers of the palest yellow through to the brightest yellows, oranges and reds are shown off to perfection.

The petals and leaves are worked in straight stitch and ribbon stitch, and time and care spent placing the stitches accurately, as shown on the template, will be well rewarded. Painting and shading brings the finished embroidery to life.

The template, half actual size; enlarge to 200 per cent. Transfer the shape of the background leaves using light pencil dots. When you have painted the background, replace the template and transfer the positions of the leaves. Draw in the connecting lines, then repeat for the flower centres, buds, points X and Z on the main stem and the points along the stem where it is intersected by a side stem; do not draw in the petal lines, apart from petals A, B and C of the background flower, 7, as they will show.

3m (118½in) 13mm Yellow (No. 15)

1m (39½in) 7mm Yellow (No. 15)

0.67m (26½in) 13mm Moss (No. 20)

1m (39½in) 13mm White (No. 03)

1m (39½in) 7mm White (No. 03)

0.5m (19¾in) 4mm Soft Yellow (No. 14)

Painting the background leaves

1 Mix yellow fabric paint and blue silk paint on a tile to make green, then to half the green add a spot of red to make a more mossy shade. Using a fine brush, lightly paint a thin line around each leaf shape as a guide, and put in the dot in the centre. Now use a small, stiff, straight-edged brush and a tiny amount of paint to lightly paint in the leaves with brushstrokes radiating out from the centre dot. Leave to dry and press.

35 x 30cm (13¾ x 11¾in) linen/cotton fabric; stranded thread in Soft Apple Green (No. 264) and a white thread to match the background fabric; deep yellow coton à broder; silk paints in poppy red, navy blue and primary yellow; fabric paints in cobalt blue, buttercup yellow, cardinal red and white.

Painting the ribbon

Note: if, when applied to the ribbon, a colour is too deep, wipe the ribbon along its length with a paper towel to remove some of the excess. More colour can always be added.

2 Cut the 13mm Yellow ribbon in half, making two 1.5m (59¼in) lengths. Put some red silk paint on to a tile and dilute it with two or three drops of water. Moisten one length of the ribbon with clean water and paint it using a stiff paintbrush, allowing the shade to vary along its length (see page 15). Hang the ribbon up to dry. Add a little more water to the mix to make a lighter shade and repeat using the other 1.5m (59¼in) length, then dye the 7mm Yellow ribbon a little paler still.

3 Mix yellow and blue silk paint to make a mid green and add a tiny spot of red to make a slightly more mossy shade, then randomly dye the 13mm White ribbon (see page 15). Make the paint slightly paler and dye the 7mm White ribbon. Dry and press all the painted ribbons.

Flowers 1 and 2

4 Cut a length of the paler orange 13mm ribbon, fold one end in half lengthwise and thread this end into a large needle (see page 22). Take the ribbon through to the back at the tip of petal A of flower 1 so that the fold is at the top (like an inverted V) and the ribbon opens out towards the centre of the flower. Remove the needle, open the ribbon out on the wrong side and secure it behind the petal about to be worked. Work a centre ribbon stitch at the base, pulling the ribbon over the eye-end of another needle to lift it and gently elongate the throat of the petal. Fasten off. Use a cotton bud to lift and shape the petal. Work petals B, C, D and E in the same way but without elongating the throat.

5 Work flower 2 in the same way.

6 Knot the end of a length of 4mm Soft Yellow ribbon and thread it into a size 18 needle. Bring the needle up at the base of petal A of flower 1 and work a centre ribbon stitch into the flower centre. Work the remaining petals and flower 2 in the same way.

Flower 3

7 Work petal A as a flatter straight stitch, and B as a centre ribbon stitch, then work petals C to E as in steps 4 and 6.

Buds

8 Use the 7mm dyed orange ribbon to work a straight stitch from the base of bud 1 to A. Fasten off and repeat for B. Fasten off.

9 Using 7mm dyed green ribbon, work a straight stitch from the base of the bud to C and repeat to D, using a second needle to wrap the stitches around the petals. Fasten off.

10 Anchor the 7mm dyed green ribbon at the base of the bud, pull it over a second needle to straighten it and twist the first 3–4cm (approx. 1½in) of the ribbon into a coil. Take the needle down through the ribbon (to hold the twist) and through the fabric at the tip of the spur. Fasten off.

11 Work bud 2 as bud 1, but with only one petal (A).

Background flower 7

12 Using the deep orange 13mm ribbon, work three straight stitches at A, B and C. Do not work the calyx.

Leaves 1, 2 and top right

Note the angle of the second needle at each end of the leaves.

13 Starting with leaf 1, anchor the 13mm dyed green ribbon at A and work a straight stitch at B. Fasten off, then work C-D so that it overlaps slightly with A-B. To pull the ribbon down and shape the leaf, use a single strand of toning thread and work a tiny stitch through the edge of both ribbons at E. Fasten off.

14 Work the four small leaves in the top right of the picture in the same way using the 7mm dyed green ribbon; use only one stitch for the two smallest leaves at the tip of the main stem.

Stems

15 Thread six strands of Soft Apple Green into a needle, make a knot 1cm (½in) from one end, then bring the needle up at the base of the main stem (X). Referring to the template, place the thread along the length of the stem and take the needle down at Z. Do not fasten off. Couch the stem in position, in line with the dots marking the intersections with the side stems. Using three strands for the flower and bud stems and two strands for the leaves, work the remaining stems as marked on the template. Use the eye-end of the needle to pass them under the leaves where necessary.

Painting the flowers

16 Mix yellow fabric paint and blue silk paint on a tile to make green then add a touch of red to make a deep brown-red. Use a clean, dry, fine-pointed brush to pick up a tiny amount of paint and lightly paint in the veins that radiate outwards from the base of petal A of flower 1. Paint the remaining petals in the same way, followed by flowers 2 and 3. Leave to dry.

17 Slightly dilute some red silk paint, moisten petal A of flower 1 from the centre up with a clean brush, and apply paint at the centre of the petal only, allowing the colour to fan out for approximately 0.5cm (¼in) and fade at the edges. Paint the remaining petals in the same way, then complete flowers 2 and 3. Leave to dry.

18 Make a deep brown-red mix as in step 16 to shade the base of each petal of flower 7. Leave to dry.

Painting the leaves

19 For leaves 1 and 2, use white fabric paint and a fine-pointed brush to paint in the fine veins radiating outwards from E (the centre point). Leave to dry. Paint the veins on the small leaves in the top right of the picture in the same way.

20 Mix two areas of mid-green silk paint on a tile and add a tiny spot of red to one to make a mossy shade. Moisten leaf 2 with clean water and apply spots of each colour at random, allowing them to fade out at the edges. Dilute the mid-green mixes and paint the remaining leaves in the same way. Allow to dry.

Completing the flowers, leaves and stems

21 Begin with the calyx of flower 7 (the background flower). Using the 7mm dyed orange ribbon, bring the needle up at D and work a straight stitch at E, pulling the ribbon over a second needle at D to make the stitch more pointed at E. Repeat for D-F.

22 For flower 4, work all the petals as for petal A of flower 1 using the deeper orange 13mm ribbon. For flowers 5 and 6, work petals A and B as straight stitches, then the remaining petals as petal A of flower 1. Work the spur as for the buds (step 10). Stitch all the flower centres following step 6.

23 Using 13mm Moss ribbon, work the remaining leaves as for leaf 1 (see step 13). Work the rest of the stems.

24 Paint in the veins on the remaining flowers following steps 16 and 17, using red silk paint diluted very slightly and a dry brush.

25 Paint the rest of the leaves following steps 19 and 20, but using a mid green and a deep green mix.

Stamens

26 Thread a length of yellow coton à broder into a needle, make a knot 1–2cm (approx. ¾in) from one end and take it down through the centre of flower 1 to leave a tail thread on the top of the fabric. Taking care not to crush the flowers, carefully tie an anchoring knot tight to the back of the fabric (see page 38). Bring the needle back through close to the first thread and form a 1cm (½in) loop on the top of the fabric. Knot the thread and repeat to make a second loop. Tie one more knot, then bring the thread back through to the right side and cut it 1cm (½in) from the fabric. Cut through the loops on the top of the fabric and trim the stamens to approximately 7mm (¼in). Work the remaining flowers in the same way.

27 Using fabric paint, make a brown-red mix and paint the tip of each stamen. Leave to dry.

All of the nasturtiums above are worked in the same way as that on page 109, except that the flowers in the centre are worked with 7mm ribbon.

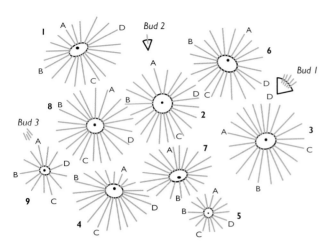

The template, half actual size; enlarge to 200 per cent. After painting the background, transfer the positions of flowers 2–5 first. Mark the flower centres and each end of the petals, then lightly draw in petal lines A to D only. Replace the template and repeat for flowers 1 and 6 to 9, and the tips of the petals of the buds. Note: some flowers have oval centres.

9m (355½in) 4mm Yellow (No. 15)

4m (158in) 2mm Moss (No. 20)

3m (118½in) 2mm Deep Green (No. 21)

33 x 28cm (13 x 11in) linen/cotton fabric; stranded threads in Deep Moss (No. 268), Moss (No. 266), Copper (No. 888), Gold (No. 306), Yellow (No. 305) and a white thread to match the background fabric; silk paints in poppy red, navy blue and primary yellow; fabric paint in buttercup yellow; 25cm (9¾in) of kitchen string.

Ursinnia

The bright yellow, orange or red flowers appear in the wild on the dry savannah of South Africa. Daisy-like flowers, with their prominent centres, sit above a mass of tiny leaves. To create the suggestion of the leaves, I rolled a short piece of string into a small coil, dipped it into the paint and used it to lightly colour the leafy background behind the flowers. The flowers were then worked in straight stitch and painted. Finally, 2mm green ribbon was used to work more leaves at random in fly stitch.

Painting the background

1 Mix yellow fabric paint and blue silk paint on a tile to make two shades of green. Wind the string round two fingers of one hand, slide the string off your fingers and hold one end of the loops firmly in your hand. Dab the loops at the other end into the paints and lightly apply colour randomly to the area where the flowers will be embroidered, creating the impression of tiny background leaves. Leave to dry and press.

Flower 1

Note: the petals vary slightly in length and their closeness to adjacent petals; refer to the template as you work. The long petals at the front and towards the sides of the oval-shaped flowers have more lift and get progressively flatter towards the back, where the petals are shorter. This suggests the tilt of the flower.

2 Thread a size 18 needle with a 50cm (19¾in) length of 4mm Yellow ribbon and knot one end. Bring the needle up at the base of petal A and, pulling the ribbon over the eye-end of a second needle, work a straight stitch at the tip. Gently pull the ribbon to elongate the tip, then bring the needle up at the base of petal B.

Work petals B, C and D in the same way, then work the remaining petals round in order and fasten off.

Note: it is important not to take the ribbons across the centre of the flower.

3 Put a little red silk paint on a tile, then with a clean, pointed brush moisten the bottom half of three or four petals. Apply a little of the red paint at the base of each petal and allow it to spread and fade out towards the tip. Paint the remaining petals in the same way and leave to dry. Now mix blue and red silk paint to make purple, clean and dry the brush, then with the tip of the brush gently paint tiny lines from the base of each petal. Leave to dry.

4 For the flower centre, thread three strands of Copper thread into a needle and knot one end. Work a three-loop French knot in the centre of the flower and fasten off. Now thread two strands of Gold and one of Yellow into a needle as before, work a ring of tightly packed two-loop French knots round the first knot, then work one-loop knots to fill the centre and complete the flower. Fasten off.

Flowers 2–9

5 Work the remaining flowers in the same way, in numerical order. Note that the petals of flower 5 are raised slightly more than those of the other flowers.

Buds

6 Work the straight stitch petals of bud 1 with 4mm Yellow ribbon and fasten off. Using 2mm Moss ribbon, work six straight stitches for the calyx, overlapping them at the base and radiating outwards to just cover the bottom of the petals. Fasten off. Work bud 2 in the same way, but with only a single straight stitch petal and five sepals. Bud 3 is worked as bud 2, but without a petal.

Stems and leaves

7 Work a short straight stitch from each bud with three strands of Deep Moss thread for the stems. The leaves are worked as random fly stitches using 2mm ribbon (see page 36). Work darker green leaves in the shaded areas then use the lighter green elsewhere. Fill in the gaps with fly stitches worked using a strand each of Moss and Deep Moss threads to complete.

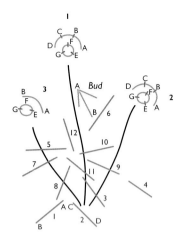

The template, half actual size; enlarge to 200 per cent. Transfer the positions of the flowers, bud, leaves and the bases of the stems. Lightly draw in leaf lines 5 to 12 only.

1.25m (49¼in) 13mm Cream (No. 156)

0.75m (29½in) 13mm Just Green (No. 31)

0.25m (9¾in) 7mm Just Green (No. 31)

0.25m (9¾in) 4mm Pale Yellow (No. 13)

Petal numbers.

30 x 30cm (11¾ x 11¾in) linen/cotton fabric; stranded thread in Green (No. 216), Pale Pink (No. 73) and a white thread to match the background fabric; silk paints in magenta, navy blue and primary yellow; fabric paints in cobalt blue and buttercup yellow.

Viola

Growing almost all the year round, the pansy is a wonderfully versatile plant and popular with gardeners. The flowers each have five petals and are often likened to painted faces. They come in a huge range of vibrant colours, from white through to blue, purple, yellow and red to almost black, either a single colour or almost any combination of colours.

Worked in 13mm cream ribbon, the back two petals are worked first and then the front three. This variety is known as Antique Surprise. I love its pale, shaded petals, but you could use any combination of colours you like.

Flower 1

Note: only cut the 13mm ribbon after the running stitches for a petal have been worked.

1 Thread a fine needle with a strand of Pale Pink thread and knot one end. Using 13mm Cream ribbon and, referring to diagrams 1 and 2 at the bottom of the facing page, work the tiny running stitches and cut the ribbon as indicated (see pages 32–33).

2 Using a strand of white thread, anchor the knot end of the shorter length of ribbon at point A, then bring the needle up at B.

3 Take the needle through point X on the ribbon and back down at B to secure it, then bring the needle up at C, avoiding the gathering thread. Fold the ribbon upwards along the gathering line X-Y. Take the needle through the fold at point Y, just above the gathering line Y-Z, and back through the fabric at C. Keep the thread to one side. Now take the end of the ribbon through the fabric at D and position it to sit the petals flat on the fabric. Use the white thread to secure the end of the ribbon behind the petals.

4 Place a finger lightly on the ribbon along the line A-D, gently pull the gathering thread so that the selvedge sits evenly on the line, then stab stitch the selvedge in place to complete petals 1 and 2. Gently pull the gathering thread to seat the petals and fasten off.

5 Anchor the longest length of stitched ribbon at E with a white thread, work a stab stitch through X and through Y to secure them at F, then gather and stitch along E-F for petal 3. Bring the needle up at G.

6 Fold the ribbon forwards along the angled gathering line, take the needle through the fold at V and down through the fabric at G. Place your finger over the ribbon as before, and gather and secure the ribbon along the line F-G to make petal 4.

7 Anchor the end of the ribbon at E to sit just in front of petal 3. Place a finger on the ribbon and gather it, then stitch it in place with the white thread as before. Fasten off. Pull the gathering thread to seat the petals and fasten off.

Flowers 2 and 3

8 Work flower 2 as flower 1. For flower 3, stitch two lengths of ribbon following diagrams 2 and 3, attach the short length of ribbon along A-B first, then work the other three petals following steps 5 to 7.

Painting the petals

Note: place your embroidery on a foam pad and, taking care not to pin through the ribbon, use glass-headed pins to hold the petals away from the ones being painted (see page 17).

9 Mix magenta with a little blue silk paint to make a purple-pink, then add a touch of yellow to make 'old rose'. Moisten petal 2 of flower 1 from the selvedge. Dilute a little of the paint to make it paler, then apply the paint along the edge. Leave to dry, then repeat for petal 2.

10 Use a deeper shade to paint petals 3 to 5 in the same way, letting each dry before painting the next.

11 Add more paint to the mix to make a slightly deeper tone, then re-moisten petal 3 and darken the base of the petal. Allow to dry, then repeat for petal 4. Deepen the shade still further and apply more paint to the base of petal 5. Leave to dry.

12 Use the deeper colour to paint an 8cm (3¼in) length of 13mm Cream ribbon for the bud. Dry and press.

Flower centres

13 Using 4mm Pale Yellow ribbon, work two loose straight stitches to fill the centre of each flower. Use yellow fabric paint to paint them a slightly deeper shade.

Bud

14 Using the piece of 13mm dyed ribbon, work a straight stitch from A at B, using the eye-end of a second needle to make the tip slightly pointed. Fasten off, then with 7mm Just Green ribbon work a reverse ribbon stitch either side for the calyx. Mix a tiny amount of magenta and blue silk paint to a deep purple, moisten the bud and paint the base of the bud. Leave to dry.

Stems

15 Referring to the template, work straight stitch stems using six strands of Green thread and couch them in place with a strand of the same colour. Leave some space for leaf 5 to sit behind.

Leaves

16 Anchor the 13mm Just Green ribbon at the base of leaf 1 at A, then using a second needle to control the ribbon, work a straight stitch at B. Fasten off. Work leaves 3 and 4 also as straight stitches, and leaves 2 and 5–9 as centre ribbon stitches. Fasten off as each is worked.

17 Mix blue and yellow fabric paint to make a deep green, then use a fine-pointed paintbrush to paint fine veins from the base to the tip of each leaf. Darken the edges of each leaf and leave to dry.

18 Moisten a leaf with clean water, dilute the paint slightly and colour the shaded areas of the leaf, leaving the raised, curved areas unpainted to suggest light and shade. Paint all the leaves, then the calyx of the bud.

19 Using three strands of Green thread, work the straight stitch stems to leaves 4, 6 and 7.

20 Work leaves 10 and 11 as ribbon stitches and 12 as a straight stitch. Paint them as before to complete the embroidery.

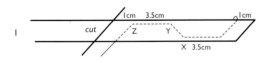

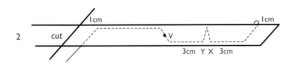

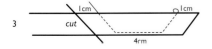

Stitching the ribbon for the flowers.

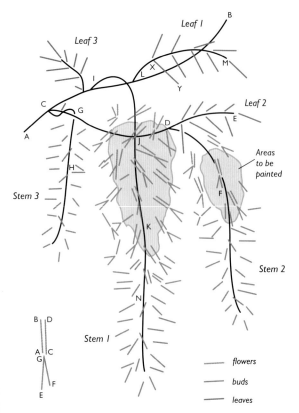

Leaf 3 · Leaf 1 · B · M · X · L · Y · Leaf 2 · E · I · C · G · D · A · H · J · F · Areas to be painted · Stem 3 · K · Stem 2 · N · B · D · A · C · G · F · E · Stem 1

—— flowers
—— buds
—— leaves

The template, half actual size; enlarge to 200 per cent.
Transfer the line of the stems A-B and C-E. Mark the side
stems where they cross over another stem and at regular
points along their length to the tip, and the outline of the
areas to be painted. When you have painted these areas,
transfer the positions of the main flowers on stems 1 and
2 (shown in purple on the template). Referring to the
diagram, lightly draw in the lines for petals A-B and C-D
and place dots only at E and F. Replace the template and
mark the positions of the leaves and the buds. Lightly draw
in the connecting lines for the buds only, not the leaves.

3m (118½in) 7mm White (No. 03)

9m (355½in) 4mm White (No. 03)

1m (39½in) 7mm Just Green (No. 31)

1m (39½in) 4mm Just Green (No. 31)

33 x 40cm (13 x 15¾in) linen/cotton fabric; stranded
thread in Just Green (No. 859), Donkey (No. 393) and a
white thread to match the background fabric; silk paints in
magenta, navy blue, primary yellow and buttercup yellow;
fabric paints in cobalt blue and buttercup yellow; 50cm
(19¾in) natural garden string.

Wisteria

This is a rampant climber, with twisting, twining often gnarled
stems bearing long racemes of showy, pea-like flowers. They are
a truly spectacular sight when trained against a wall, over an
archway or climbing up through a tree.

Although not immediately visible, the fabric behind the
main part of the flower is painted to create more depth, and
the ribbons are painted randomly in three shades of purple
before embroidering. The flowers are worked with 4 and 7mm
ribbon using a mixture of straight stitches, ribbon stitches and
lazy daisy stitch, with string used for the stems. The fully open
flowers are then shaded to complete the embroidery.

Stems

1 Moisten a piece of soap and wet
the string, then pull the soap along the
length of string several times to coat it
well all over. Leave to dry.

2 Cut a 14cm (5½in) length of string,
then partly untwist to loosen it and
couch it in position along A-B using a
matching thread.

3 Cut another 14cm (5½in) length
of string and place the end under the
main stem A-B at C. Almost completely
untwist the string to make three strands.
Leave a strand at C and take two to D,
then divide them and take one to E and
one to F. Cut the ends at an angle at E
and F and couch both stems in position.
Take the strand remaining at C in front
of and then behind the stem at G and
down to H. Cut it to length and couch in
place at G.

4 Untwist and divide the third piece of
string. Place two ends behind the main
stem at I, cut one the length of I-K and
couch it in place from just above J to K.
Cut and couch the other strand through
the centre of leaf 3. Add one more
strand, taking it in front of the main stem
as before, for L-M.

5 Make up a stem thread with two Just
Green and one brown strand, knot one
end and bring the needle up at K. Take
one green strand through to the back
at N and the remaining two strands at
the tip of the stem. Couch the threads
in place, then fasten off all the threads.
Work the ends of stems 2 and 3 in the
same way.

Painting the background

6 Mix yellow and blue fabric paint to
make a deep green then lightly paint
parts of the string stems along their
length to shade. Leave to dry.

7 Using blue and magenta silk paint,
mix two shades of purple. Using a small,
stiff, straight-edged paintbrush, apply
small areas of paint randomly within the
marked area and fade them out towards
the edges. Leave to dry.

Painting the ribbons

8 In a small bowl, mix a little magenta
and a touch of blue silk paint, and dilute
to make a very pale pinky purple. Use
it to randomly paint the 7mm White
ribbon (see page 15).

9 Cut the 4mm White ribbon into
one 3m (118½in) and three 2m (79in)
lengths. Mix magenta and blue silk paints
to make two shades of pale purple.
Moisten the 3m (118½in) length with
water then, with a stiff brush, paint it
randomly leaving some areas free of
paint. Leave to dry. Add more paint to
the mixes to make the colours a little
deeper and paint a 2m (79in) length in
the same way. Leave to dry. Make the
two mixes deeper still and paint another
2m (79in) length, leave to dry, then
add a little more magenta to one of the
mixes and paint the last length with the
more contrasting tones. Leave to dry.

10 Mix blue and yellow silk paint to
make two shades of green. Put the 7mm
and 4mm Just Green ribbons together,
moisten them and paint them randomly
with both colours, leaving some areas
free of paint. Leave to dry. Iron all the
ribbons before starting to sew.

Stem 1

Note: when stitching the flowers, start in the centre at the top of the stem and work outwards and downwards, stitching the flowers alternately from side to side.

11 Cut a length of 7mm dyed purple ribbon and anchor it at A on the diagram. Work a right ribbon stitch at B, using the eye-end of a second needle to shape the tip. Bring the needle up at C and work a straight stitch at D, placing it so that it sits under the rolled edge of the first stitch. Fasten off.

Note: always work a right ribbon stitch on the left side of a flower and, for two or three flowers, a left ribbon stitch on the right side; that way, the point where the needle goes down through the edge of the ribbon is always in the centre of the flower.

Note: four shades of 4mm dyed purple ribbon are used to work the small petals at the base of the main petals – use the deepest shades in the central part of the stem, and the two paler colours towards the outer parts to suggest light and shade.

Do not take the ribbon across the back of the fabric; work stitches that are very close together and fasten off frequently.

12 Referring to the template and using one of the 4mm dyed purple ribbons, bring the needle up at E and work a fairly loose lazy daisy stitch, taking the needle down at F and anchoring the loop at G (see page 35). Fasten off.

13 Work the remaining flowers on stem 1 that are marked on the template in purple.

14 All the buds are straight stitches worked from the base to the tip. Fill the upper part of the stem, referring to the picture for guidance, and work those lower down as marked on the template. Tuck some stitches under the main flowers. Fasten off frequently; do not take the ribbon across the back of the embroidery. Vary the shades of ribbon used, becoming progressively paler as you move down the stem.

15 Thread a fine needle with a strand each of Just Green and brown, knot one end then work straight stitch stems to connect each bud to the main stem. Do not pull the stitches too tight.

Painting the flowers

16 Painting one flower at a time, slightly dilute a little buttercup yellow silk paint, moisten the centre of the large double petals then apply a touch of colour at the base with the point of a fine brush. Leave to dry.

17 Mix a little magenta with a touch of blue silk paint and dilute to make pale pink-mauve. Moisten then paint the outer edge of each large petal. Leave to dry. Paint the remaining flowers.

Completing the stems

18 Work stems 2 and 3 as stem 1.

Leaves

Note: lift the leaves along the lower edge a little higher to suggest tilting. Fasten off as each stitch is worked.

19 For leaf 1, anchor a length of 7mm dyed green ribbon at X and work a ribbon stitch at Y. Work the remaining stitches on the right side of the leaf, including the one at the tip, in the same way. Fasten off. Work the opposite side of the leaf as straight stitches, starting at the base of the leaf. Fasten off. Work leaf 2 in the same way.

20 Work leaf 3 as leaf 1 using 4mm dyed green ribbon. Fasten off. Work the three tiny ribbon stitches at the bases of stem 3, leaf 1 and leaf 3.

21 Make a deep green with yellow fabric paint and blue silk paint. Do not dilute it. With a fine-pointed brush, paint in the fine veins on each leaf. Leave to dry.

The template, half actual size; enlarge to 200 per cent.

For this wisteria, garden string is untwisted and couched on to the fabric first and then a little green paint is very lightly applied with a sponge to suggest background leaves. Two 1.5m (60in) lengths of 4mm pink ribbon are randomly painted two different tones of purple. The flowers are embroidered in small ribbon stitches that get progressively smaller towards the tip of the flower stem, with some pale green thread stitches at the very end of some flowers for unopened buds. The leaves are also ribbon stitches, worked randomly in two shades of 4mm green ribbon.

Xeranthemum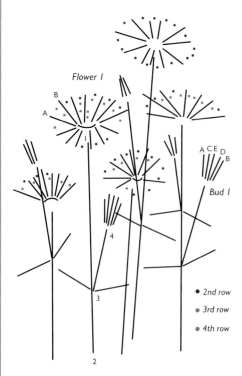

Commonly called everlasting flower, these brilliantly coloured flowers with their papery petals can be cut, hung up to dry and used for winter decoration without losing their colour. They produce masses of flowers and are the brightest of all everlasting flowers, which range from white and pale pink to the most vibrant of pinks, purples and reds.

These flowers are worked in ribbon stitch with 4mm lilac ribbon which has been dyed randomly, dried and then dyed again to create an intense colour and high degree of shading. This is an easy flower to embroider, but remember to stitch the petals round in order and never to take the ribbon across the centre of the flower.

Flower 1

Bud 1

- 2nd row
- 3rd row
- 4th row

The template, half actual size; enlarge to 200 per cent. Transfer the positions of the stems, leaves, buds and petals (just those shown by a line and a dark pink dot only). Lightly draw in the petal lines marked on the template.

7m (276½in) 4mm Just Lilac (No. 83)

1m (39½in) 4mm Sage (No. 74)

1m (39½in) 4mm Just Green (No. 31)

30 x 35cm (11¾ x 13¾in) linen/cotton fabric; stranded threads in Just Green (No. 859), Green (No. 216), Sand (No. 854), Pale Yellow (No. 292) and a white thread to match the background fabric; silk paints in raspberry, navy blue and primary yellow.

Painting the ribbon for the flowers

1 Cut a 1m (39½in) length of 4mm Just Pink ribbon and keep it to one side.

2 Moisten the remaining length of 4mm Just Pink ribbon, put some raspberry silk paint on a tile (do not dilute) and paint the ribbon very patchily (see page 15). Dry, press and paint the ribbon again in the same way. Dry and press.

Flowers

3 Start with flower 1. Cut a length of dyed pink ribbon, thread it into a large needle and knot one end. Bring the needle up at the base of petal A and work a centre ribbon stitch at the tip, keeping the ribbon fairly flat to the fabric. Bring the needle up at the base of petal B and continue to work the petals round the flowerhead that are marked as a line on the template.

4 Work the second row of petals, as shown in dark pink on the template. Bring the needle up each time between the petals in the first row, and as each petal is worked lift the tip with the point of a needle to sit it slightly above the first row.

5 Work row 3. Bring the needle up in the middle of the curved line and, referring to the template for where to place the tip, work the middle petal as a centre ribbon stitch. Use the point of a needle to lift the tip of the petal as before. Work the remaining petals in row 3 alternately from side to side.

6 Bring the needle up just below row 3 and work row 4 in the same way. Fasten off.

7 Work the rest of the flowers.

Buds

8 Using the 4mm Just Pink (not dyed) ribbon, bring the needle up at the base of petal A of bud 1 and work a straight stitch at the tip. Gently pull the ribbon slightly on the wrong side to extend the stitch and make the petal slightly pointed. Work the remaining petals in the order indicated on the template. Work the rest of the buds.

9 For the calyxes, use 4mm Sage ribbon. Bring the needle up at the top of the stem and work the middle leaf of the calyx as a ribbon stitch, taking the needle down through the base of a petal. Work another ribbon stitch either side at a slight angle. Fasten off.

Stems

10 Make a thread with three strands of Just Green and one of Green and thread it into a needle. Knot one end. Bring the needle up at 1 (at the base of flower 1) and work a straight stitch at 2, then bring the needle up at 3 and down again at 4. Fasten off. Work the remaining stems in the same way.

Leaves

11 Mix blue and yellow silk paint to make a deep blue-green, moisten the 4mm Just Green ribbon and paint it patchily (see page 15). Leave to dry and press.

12 Knot the end of a length of the dyed green ribbon, bring the needle up at the base of a leaf and work a ribbon stitch at the tip. Fasten off then work the remaining leaves to complete the embroidery.

Flower centre

13 Using a strand each of Sand, Pale Yellow and Just Green thread, work a cluster of three two-loop French knots in the middle of the flower at the top, then work one-loop French knots around it to fill the flower centre.

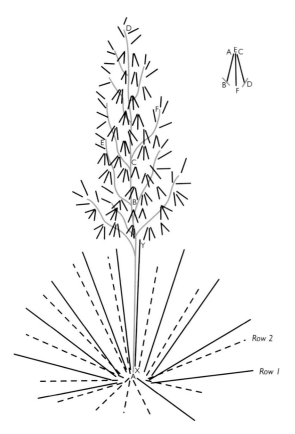

Row 2

Row 1

The template, half actual size; enlarge to 200 per cent. Using light dots, transfer the positions of the stems and leaves, then very lightly draw in the bottom 3cm (1¼in) only of those leaves marked with a solid line on the template (otherwise the pencil lines will show). When you have painted the background and stitched the stems, replace the template and transfer the flowers and buds of alternate stems. Lift the template and very lightly draw these in. Now replace the template and repeat for the remaining flowers and buds.

5m (197½in) 4mm White (No. 03)

2m (79in) 4mm Soft Green (No. 33)

4m (158in) 4mm Just Green (No. 31)

35 x 40cm (13¾ x 15¾in) linen/cotton fabric; stranded thread in Soft Apple Green (No. 264) and a white thread to match the background fabric; silk paints in navy blue, primary yellow and poppy red; fabric paint in lemon yellow.

Yucca

Thriving in full sunlight, the yucca can be found growing wild in parts of the world where it is hot and dry, such as sand dunes and deserts. It is eye-catching from every angle, with its strong, straight, pointed leaves radiating out from a central stem topped with white, bell-shaped flowers.

To give depth to the embroidery, some background leaves have been painted on to the fabric before working the long ribbon stitch leaves. The flowers are then formed from straight stitches worked either side of a centre ribbon stitch; vary which stitches you work first to give a sense of movement to the piece.

Painting the background and the stem thread

1 Mix blue silk paint and yellow fabric paint to make two shades of green – a mid-green and a blue-green. Using the side of the brush, paint each leaf starting from the base of the stem and tapering towards the tip. Begin by putting in a few leaves as a guide and gradually add more, all radiating out randomly from the base of the stem and with the tips just above and below the marked leaves.

2 Wrap the Soft Apple Green thread around two fingers, then put the rolled-up thread on a tile and dab it all over with both green mixes. Leave small areas without paint on them; moisten these areas so the colour blends into them. Unwind the thread and suspend to dry.

Painting the ribbon

3 Mix blue and yellow silk paint to make a yellow-green, then add a little red to make brown. Dilute the mix with water to make a very pale cream and test the colour on a piece of white paper. Moisten the 4mm White ribbon and paint it randomly to very lightly colour it (see page 15). Leave to dry, then press.

4 For the leaf ribbon, mix blue and yellow silk paint to make a mid-green and a darker blue-green. Moisten the 4mm Just Green and the 4mm Soft Green ribbon and dye them randomly. Leave to dry then press.

Stems

5 Cut two 30cm (11¾in) lengths of dyed green thread, separate all the strands and put ten back together to make a stem thread. Knot one end and thread it into a needle. Moisten the thread with clean water then rub a piece of soap along 15cm (6in) of it from the knot end.

6 Bring the needle up at A and couch all the strands to B. Leave three strands to one side and couch the rest to C. Again, put three strands to one side and take the remaining four strands down at D. Couch them in place and fasten off.

7 Thread the three strands at B into a needle and take them down at E. Couch them in place and fasten off. Similarly, couch the strands at C to F and fasten off.

8 Work the remaining stems using three strands, fastening off the thread as each stem is worked.

Flowers and buds

Note: work all the flowers and buds on the lowest stem on the left first, fasten off, then work those on the next stem up on the right. Continue up the plant, finishing with those at the top. Place some flowers and buds under the stems as shown in the picture. Use the 4mm dyed cream ribbon.

Work clusters of flowers and buds that are close together and fasten off frequently to avoid taking any ribbon across the back of the work.

9 For the flowers that consist of three petals, bring the needle up at A shown on the diagram and work a straight stitch at B. Use the eye-end of a second needle to guide the ribbon. Repeat for C–D. Work E–F as a centre ribbon stitch to sit over the first two stitches. Fasten off. Work the buds as single straight stitches.

10 When you have completed all the flowers and buds, use a single strand of the stem thread to work straight stitches (not too tightly) to connect each flower and bud to the stems (refer to the picture for where to place these).

Leaves

Note: all the leaves are left, right and centre ribbon stitches, worked mainly with a single twist in the ribbon. Fasten off each leaf as it is worked.

11 Thread a length of 4mm Soft Green ribbon into a needle and knot one end. Bring the needle up at X, twist the ribbon once then work a centre ribbon stitch at Y. Fasten off. Work the remaining leaves in row 1 marked on the template.

12 Using the 4mm green dyed ribbon, work the second row of leaves, then work more shorter leaves to gradually fill in the central area.

Flower 1

Flower 2

—— needle angles

The template, half actual size; enlarge to 200 per cent. Transfer the positions of the stems and the dots of both petals.

1.5m (59¼in) 32mm White (No. 03)

35 x 40cm (13¾ x 15¾in) linen/cotton fabric; 10 x 10cm (4 x 4in) thin wadding; stranded thread in Just Green (No. 859), Yellow (No. 305) and a white thread to match the background fabric; silk paints in navy blue and primary yellow; 25cm (9¾in) tubular cord, 4–5mm (¼in) diameter; 44cm (17¼in) of 22 gauge paper-covered wire; 2cm (¾in) wide adhesive tape; clear silicone or PVA glue; small screw-top jar; pith board.

Zantedeschia

Liking moist, damp soil, arum lilies are often found growing round the edges of ponds, but in the wild can be seen on dry slopes in both North and South America. They are the most elegant and regal of flowers, facing up towards the sky like a fanfare of trumpets and balanced by a mass of bright green leaves beneath. The single white spathe (not a petal) is in fact a continuation of the stem.

The stem and yellow centre (spadix) is worked over a wire and covered with a cord before working the ribbon. Two lengths of 32mm ribbon are then used to work the stem and the wide spathe that opens out in one continuous and smooth line. Take time with this flower, the result is well worthwhile.

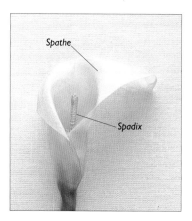

Spathe

Spadix

Preparing the stems and spadix

1 Begin with stem 1 (stem 2 can be made after step 9). Cut a 22cm (8¾in) length of wire and use the tip of the pliers to bend over the top 2.8cm (1in), then bend the wire at a slight angle 3cm (1¼in) from the top. Apply a little glue to the bend in the wire (see diagram A).

2 Using a 50cm (19¾in) length of Yellow thread, leave a 10cm (4in) tail and wrap it around the glued section five or six times. Now bend the covered part of the wire over so that the bound area is at the top (see diagram B). Press the three wires at the top of the stem together with the pliers, then continue wrapping them tightly and smoothly with the Yellow thread to form the spadix. Tie off the threads. Do not glue, but lay another thread with a tail and wrap as before. Tie off and cut the threads short.

3 Apply a little glue to the wire immediately below the spadix, then thread the wire through the centre of the cord leaving the spadix protruding from the top. Press to secure the cord to the wire.

4 Cut a 14cm (5½in) length of sticky tape and wrap it tightly, at an angle, around the cord to prevent the ridges on the cord from showing through once the stem is covered by the ribbon.

5 Cut a piece of wadding, 10 x 4cm (4 x 1½in). Apply a little glue to the top of the stem, just below the spadix. Attach the short edge of the wadding to the stem to just cover the base of the yellow thread and wrap it firmly round twice. Twist it once and finish wrapping it to form the bulbous area at the base of the flower. Use a white thread to sew a few tiny stitches through at the base of the wadding, then wind it round tightly two or three times to secure the wadding to the stem and fasten off.

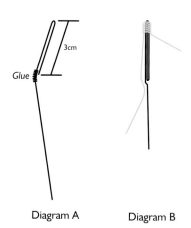

Diagram A   Diagram B

Flower 1

Note: avoid creasing the ribbon at all times.

6 Cut two lengths of 32mm White ribbon – an 18cm (7in) length and a 26cm (10¼in) length. Cut both ends of each at the same angle, so they are parallel to each other. Press both lengths. Prepare a mix of blue and yellow silk paint to make green as a base colour and test it on a spare piece of ribbon. Store it in a small pot with a lid.

7 Beginning with the ribbon forming the right side of the spathe, place the 18cm (7in) ribbon lengthways on a pith board. Lay the stem on top, with the tip of the spadix 11cm (4¼in) from the top of the ribbon. Position the spadix centrally so that its best side is uppermost. Place a pin through the wadding, the ribbon and into the board to hold it securely.

8 Wrap both sides of the ribbon firmly over the wadding, laying the left side over the right and crossing the ribbons over 1.5cm (¾in) down from the top edge of the wadding. Using a white thread, place two or three stitches at the cross-over to secure the ribbon. Remove the pin and lift the stem, then wrap the ribbon tightly and smoothly round to the back. Slip stitch it in place down the back of the stem to secure. Fasten off.

_9_ Place the stem on the pith board with the back of the spathe uppermost and the spadix and the ribbon over the edge of the board. Place a pin through the top of the stem below the wadding to hold it in position. Place the board on the edge of a table so that the ribbon hangs free, and place a weight on it to prevent it moving. Moisten the entire length of the ribbon and paint the stem to just below the bulbous area using the paint you mixed earlier (see step 6). Now, holding it up and away from the wadding, apply paint to the bulbous area. Dilute the paint slightly and paint the padded area up to the base of the spadix. Dilute it slightly again and paint a further 1cm (½in) of the ribbon. Position the pith board so that the ribbon hangs down without touching anything and leave it to dry.

_10_ While you are waiting for the ribbon to dry, make the stem and spadix of flower 2 (see steps 1–5).

_11_ Begin forming the left side of the spathe of flower 1. Place the 26cm (10¼in) ribbon lengthways on the pith board and lay the painted stem on top 1cm (½in) from the left edge of the ribbon, as shown in diagram C. Put two glass-headed pins through the middle of the stem and into the board to hold it in place. Remove the pins and wrap the ribbon around the stem, again laying the left side over the right so that the cross-over point is on the back of the left part of the spathe and about 1cm (½in) below the cross-over point of the first ribbon. Continue wrapping the ribbon round and anchor it to the back of the flower in the middle, about 1cm (½in) lower still; the width of the ribbon should sit smoothly across the front of the flower. Slip stitch along the back of the stem taking care not to pucker the ribbon. Fasten off.

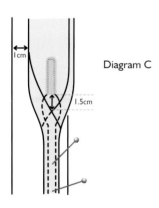

Diagram C

Note: the cross-over of the left part of spathe should be on the right and that of the right part of the spathe on the left.

_12_ Paint the left part of the spathe as you did the right part.

_13_ Iron each part of the spathe carefully from the tip down to the stem. Be careful not to crease the ribbon as you work, or leave the impression of the iron.

_14_ Place the flower on the background fabric and check that the two ribbons overlap at the back and that the wadding is obscured at the

front. Adjust them if necessary, then pin the back of the stem in place through the back of the fabric using two glass-headed pins. Working on the wrong side, attach the flower to the background fabric using slip stitches placed at regular intervals down the back of the stem, hiding the stitch line. Fasten off, trim the base of the stem and leave it unstitched.

_15_ Using a size 13 needle, carefully make a hole through the weave of the fabric at A. Do not thread the ribbon into a needle at this stage. Practise shaping the spathe by taking the right ribbon and rolling it loosely over the eye-end of a size 13 needle placed approximately 1cm (½in) above point A at the angle marked on the template. Make sure that the left edge of the spathe sits slightly to the left of the spadix.

_16_ Repeat step 15 but this time thread the ribbon into a size 13 needle and take it down through the fabric at A. Pull the ribbon over a second large needle out towards the left on the wrong side of the fabric to create a raised, curved spathe with the left edge placed just left of the spadix and the right edge rolled underneath smoothly as in the picture. Secure the ribbon using a white thread, making sure it still lies out to the left.

_17_ Practise forming spathe 2 as you did spathe 1 (step 15), this time making the hole at B. Thread the ribbon into the needle and create

the spathe, taking the end of the ribbon out to the right and securing it. Make sure the right selvedge of the ribbon sits exactly in line with the left selvedge of spathe 1 with no gaps.

Flower 2

_18_ Work as flower 1, but note that points A and B are on opposite sides of the flower. Work the left part of the spathe first, laying the ribbon out to the left and pulling to the right on the wrong side of the fabric while at the same time making sure that the right edge of the ribbon sits behind the spadix as before. When working the right part of the spathe, lay the ribbon back and downwards in line with the stem to create the rolled edge; make sure this sits alongside the edge of the first spathe to create a continuous line and therefore a single spathe.

These calla lilies are smaller and easier to work than the arum lily; the spathe is worked with one length of 32mm ribbon and wrapped around a slightly smaller spadix. Worked in white ribbon, these flowers become simply smaller versions of the arum lily.

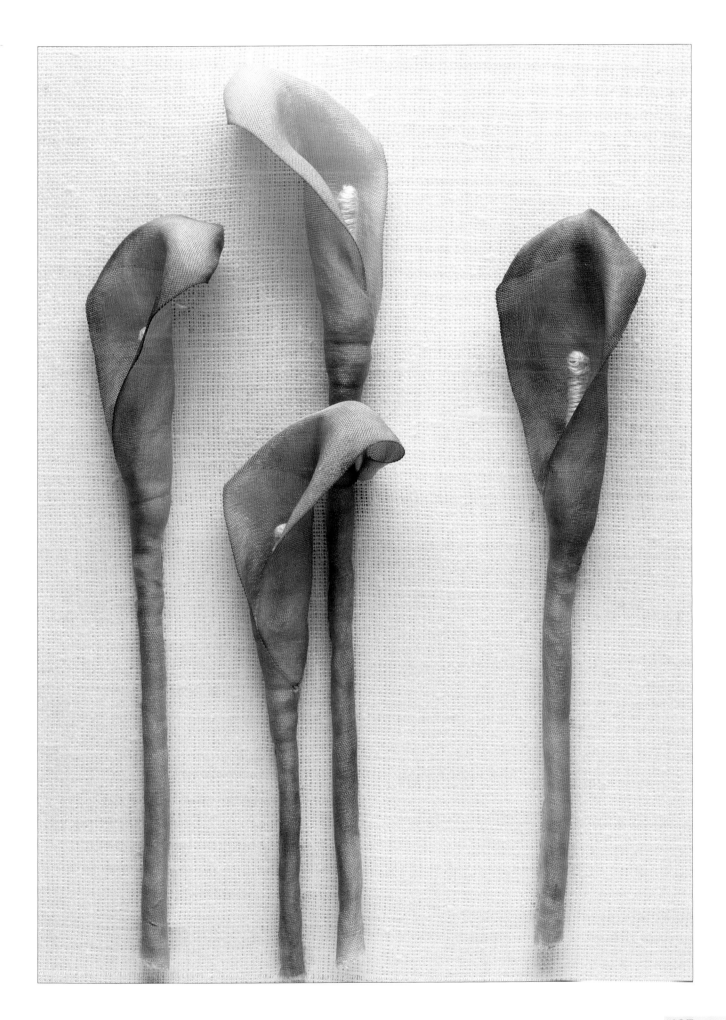